To:

Saul and Linh
on you Wedding Day

From:

Your Parents

Bolivar and Silvia
with Love

September 27, 2008

Requests for information should be addressed to:
    Inspirio, the Gift Group of Zondervan
    Grand Rapids, Michigan 49530

Senior Editor: Gwen Ellis
Project Editor: Pat Matuszak
Design By: Chris Gannon

Printed in China
02 03 04 05 / HK / 5 4 3

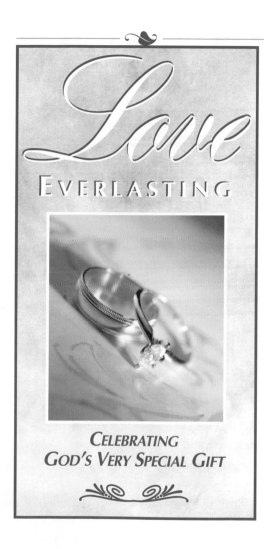

Love

EVERLASTING

**CELEBRATING
GOD'S VERY SPECIAL GIFT**

BOK5063

Contents

Getting Off on the Right Foot

Words of Life for a Marriage

Only You

My Best Friend

Wisdom Becomes You

Having Fun

Loving Through Thick and Thin

Getting Off

ON THE

Right Foot

Building THE
FRAMEWORK OF YOUR MARRIAGE
ON *God's* SOLID GROUND

*W*hen Jesus Christ laid down his life, he gave us the perfect example of what love is all about. Couples who look to him as an example, grow into an understanding of what it means to prefer one another in love. Having a fifty-fifty relationship, putting the other person first, or going the extra mile, are nice phrases to use when talking about relationships. But when it comes to putting these good intentions into practice, we find out what a strong hold our own selfish interests have on our hearts and minds.

We can only give God's kind of unconditional and unselfish love as he gives us his empowering strength. The good news is that we can come to God and ask for strength and help as often as we like —even if it seems like we need it several times a day! Just remember, God's miracles can happen in everyday life. They can happen in a kitchen as quickly as they can in a cathedral. He is everpresent to help us and he alone has the ability to smooth out the wrinkles and remove the spots that stain our relationships.

*O*ur faith in God is the foundation for our marriage. We define our marriage as a partnership with each other and with God. Years ago we chose Ecclesiastes 4:9-12 as a theme for our marriage. It describes what we want our marriage relationship to look like:

"Two are better than one, because they have a good return for their work: If one falls down, his friend can help him up. But pity the man who falls and has no one to help him up! Also, if two lie down together, they will keep warm. But how can one keep warm alone? Though one may be overpowered, two can defend themselves. A cord of three strands is not quickly broken."

—David & Claudia Arp

*F*or every house is built by someone, but God is the builder of everything.

—*Hebrews 3:4*

Jesus gave this example:

Who comes to me and hears my words and puts them into practice. . . . is like a man building a house, who dug down deep and laid the foundation on rock. When a flood came, the torrent struck that house but could not shake it, because it was well built.

—*Luke 6:47-48*

It is important for you to understand that the love you feel for each other needs to be grounded in agape love. This love is *Absolute* love and comes directly from God; there is no substitute for it, and you could never crank it out on your own.... We have, then, two loves that merge into one to bless our life together; *absolute* love and *belonging* love. Both need to be at the heart of a relationship.

—Ed Wheat

What a difference it makes in a marriage when both partners can turn to God and find that He is "a refuge and strength, a present help in time of need."

—Bill & Lynne Hybels

*T*his is how we know what love is: Jesus Christ laid down his life for us.

—*1 John 3:16*

*M*arriage is a good thing. Marriage blesses. Marriage is that mysterious, spiritual fusion of two separate lives headed in two separate directions into one flesh.

—Patrick Morley

"*F*or I know the plans I have for you," declares the Lord, "plans to prosper you and not to harm you, plans to give you a hope and a future."

—*Jeremiah 29:11*

*L*ove is also, in my view, the meaning of all human adventure. The instinct which God gave man in creating him in his own image is in fact, I believe, an instinct of love, a need to give himself, to dedicate himself, to pursue a worthwhile goal, accepting sacrifice in order to attain it.

—Paul Tournier

*U*nless the LORD builds the house, its builders labor in vain. Unless the LORD watches over the city, the watchmen stand guard in vain. In vain you rise early and stay up late, toiling for food to eat—for he grants sleep to those he loves.

—Psalm 127:1-2

*Y*our feelings are neither all-powerful nor all-wise. You can appreciate them as indicators—the things that let you know what's happening to you—but never as infallible guides. Only God's Word, the Bible, can guide us surely.

—Ed Wheat

*L*et the word of Christ dwell in you richly as you teach and admonish one another with all wisdom, and as you sing psalms, hymns and spiritual songs with gratitude in your hearts to God.

—Colossians 3:16

*F*aith is unutterable trust in God, trust which never dreams that He will not stand by us.

—Oswald Chambers

*T*rue romantic love seems to open a lover's eyes to see the loved one the way God sees that person—as extraordinary, priceless, like no one else ever created, as unique with an eternal identity.

—Ed Wheat

*H*is compassions never fail. They are new every morning; great is your faithfulness.

—*Lamentations 3:22-23*

*F*ollow the way of love.

—*1 Corinthians 14:1*

*I*n the book of Ecclesiastes, Solomon penned some of the most exquisite wisdom literature ever conceived. The message of Ecclesiastes is clear: Apart from God life has no meaning.

—Patrick Morley

*C*lothe yourselves with the Lord Jesus Christ.

—*Romans 13:14*

*T*hey will grow like a cedar of Lebanon; planted in the house of the LORD, they will flourish in the courts of our God. They will still bear fruit in old age, they will stay fresh and green, proclaiming, "The LORD is upright; he is my Rock."

—Psalm 92:12–15

*B*e devoted to one another in brotherly love. Honor one another above yourselves. Never be lacking in zeal, but keep your spiritual fervor, serving the Lord. Be joyful in hope, patient in affliction, faithful in prayer.

—Romans 12:10–12

*P*eacemakers who sow in peace raise a harvest of righteousness.

—James 3:18

*F*or you were once darkness, but now you are light in the Lord. Live as children of light (for the fruit of the light consists in all goodness, righteousness and truth) and find out what pleases the Lord.

—Ephesians 5:8–10

*B*lessed is the man who does not walk in the counsel of the wicked or stand in the way of sinners or sit in the seat of mockers. But his delight is in the law of the LORD, and on his law he meditates day and night. He is like a tree planted by streams of water, which yields its fruit in season and whose leaf does not wither. Whatever he does prospers.

—*Psalm 1:1–3*

*N*o one ... does everything right! You may know all there is to know about marriage enrichment, but that is not a passport to marital success. It's the daily grinding it out. Making unselfish choices, forgiving and asking for forgiveness, and giving each other grace—that's what helps us maintain a healthy marriage. It's choosing daily to grow together.

"If you play it safe in life," says Shirley Hufstedler, "you've decided that you don't want to grow anymore." But the secret of growing is getting started. ... Remember, marriage is a journey, not a destination—and no one ever arrives.

—David & Claudia Arp

Communication

As couples we talk things over. We talk about, around, and through all the stuff of our life together. Sometimes we feel that we will never get to the end of all our words. We wonder if the other person will ever get it—will ever understand our thoughts in the way we try to express them. But as we continue to talk to each other, we learn that persistence and patience can bring us to a wonderful moment of aha—and finally, we know we've reached an understanding. Oh joy! Can anything be better? Our eyes meet. They light up with that special light and we know we will always remember this moment, especially when we come to another passage—another time when we need to talk things out again.

Grant that we may not so much seek to be understood as to understand.

—Saint Francis of Assisi

*G*ood communication is a decision.

—Patrick Morley

*J*esus said,
"The good man brings good things out of the
good stored up in his heart. ... For out of the over-
flow of his heart his mouth speaks."

—*Luke 6:45*

*T*he belief in a happily-ever-after marriage is
one of the most widely held and destructive marriage myths.

—Drs. Les & Leslie Parrott

*O*ur marriage is still very much in process.
Something is always in flux. Family dynamics
change, situations change, and life is a continual
adjustment.... Marriages are fluid. A marriage is
either going forward or backward; standing still is
not an option.

—David & Claudia Arp

*W*omen enjoy the process of communicating as much as the results of communicating. Men are typically not like that. Men want to get to the bottom line and move on.

—Patrick Morley

*L*earn to express your feelings through loving attitudes, warmth, empathy, and sincerity.

—Gary Smalley

*I*mprove communication ... by making a life-long commitment to be "best friends." Underscore this commitment by studying the Bible and praying together, and possibly working through a couples' devotional book.

The building stage is a hectic season of accumulation, expansion, and starting and raising a family. For the husband it is the time of his greatest strength, but also the season that consumes the greatest amount of his energy.

—Patrick Morley

*M*en and women are TOTALLY different. The differences—emotionally, mentally, and physically—are so extreme that if a husband and wife don't put forth a *concentrated effort* to gain a realistic understanding of each other, it is nearly impossible for them to have a happy marriage.

—Gary Smalley

*T*hen those who feared the LORD talked with each other, and the LORD listened and heard. A scroll of remembrance was written in his presence concerning those who feared the LORD and honored his name.

—*Malachi 3:16*

*N*o one has ever seen God; but if we love one another, God lives in us and his love is made complete in us.

—*1 John 4:12*

*L*ove does no harm to its neighbor. Therefore love is the fulfillment of the law.

—*Romans 13:10*

*W*hoever of you loves life and desires to see many good days, keep your tongue from evil and your lips from speaking lies.

—*Psalm 34:12-13*

*W*hen I was a child, I talked like a child, I thought like a child, I reasoned like a child. When I became a man, I put childish ways behind me.

—*1 Corinthians 13:11*

*O*ne wonders what would be the effect if the same amount of time, energy, and money spent on the ceremony was invested in the marriage. Planning the perfect wedding too often takes precedence over planning a successful marriage.

—*Drs. Les & Leslie Parrott*

*L*et the peace of Christ rule in your hearts, since as members of one body you were called to peace. And be thankful.

—*Colossians 3:15*

*S*he feels the need for intimacy—emotional connectedness; he desires to be significant—to make a difference. Wives speak to give shape and form to what they are feeling inside; husbands speak to transfer information.

—Patrick Morley

*S*tudies of communication between husbands and wives have proven that words alone are responsible for only 7 percent of the total communication. Thirty-eight percent of marital communication is expressed through voice tone, and 55 percent through facial expressions and body movement.

—Gary Smalley

*F*orgive whatever grievances you may have against one another. Forgive as the Lord forgave you. And over all these virtues put on love, which binds them all together in perfect unity.

—*Colossians 3:13-14*

I thank my God every time I remember you. ...
I always pray with joy because of your partnership in the gospel from the first day until now,
being confident of this, that he who began a good
work in you will carry it on to completion until
the day of Christ Jesus. It is right for me to feel
this way about all of you, since I have you in my
heart.

—*Philippians 1:3–7*

I am ever struck by the tranquillity in which
Christ walked along, always having time to speak
with a poor woman beside a well, or replying to
the stupid questions of his disciples on the very
eve of his passion. To exercise a spiritual ministry
means to take time.

—Paul Tournier

T he principle that "A gentle answer turns away
wrath" (Proverbs 15:1) really works as long as
your soft answer is not said with a self-righteous
or sarcastic attitude.

—Gary Smalley

$\mathcal{O}$ne of the goals of marriage is intimacy—emotional and physical. The key to both is communication. Spouses cannot become soul mates, nor enjoy the fullness of physical lovemaking, without a deep and accurate knowledge of one another.

—Bill & Lynne Hybels

$\mathcal{L}$ift up holy hands in prayer, without anger or disputing.

—*1 Timothy 2:8*

$\mathcal{L}$earn to listen deeply without giving an overly quick reply. Be a consoler, not a consultant.

—Patrick Morley

$\mathcal{M}$ost of the time, our reaction to our mate's perceived shortcomings is worse than whatever it was our mate did or did not do. The next time you sense irritation rising, try to turn the situation around by replacing your negative response with loving encouragement for your spouse. Choose to verbalize something positive to your mate each day.

—David & Claudia Arp

Consider this: Every living person, man or woman, is good at communication about what's interesting to them. Women can talk to women, and men can talk to men. What's needed is for husbands to take a special interest in what animates their wives. Wives, of course, also need to make sure they're interested in the things that fascinate their husbands.

—Patrick Morley

God fashioned us to face life one day at a time. In his goodness, he gives us grace and help for each day. Although we may have some notion of what lies ahead, it is up to God to faithfully fill in the blanks. We are not to worry about tomorrow, only to abide in Christ today, to pray for our "daily bread." God knows our frail frame and understands we can handle only so much. Daily we are to trust in his goodness and depend on him for the wisdom and strength we need. Don't fret that you don't know it all. You really don't want to, do you? That's God's job description, and he is the only one who can fulfill it. He will tell you what you need to know, when you need it.

—Charles Stanley

*S*olitude is an indispensable aspect of a healthy marriage. An hour alone in a library or a leisurely walk can provide needed time to reflect, time to dream, even time to grow spiritually.

But there are valid reasons why it's not that easy. For one thing, the very nature of marriage is togetherness. And it is sometimes difficult to balance this yearning to experience life together with that basic need for solitude. However, good marriages don't restrict you from continuing to grow. And often that growth requires time away from each other. Ethicist Lewis B. Smedes has written of the need for couples to allow each other to be who they are—to trust each other enough to let go. That's what we do when we protect each other's private moments. We relinquish control in favor of allowing our loved one to retain those characteristics that attracted us in the first place.

Maybe it's time for spouses to admit they harbor a strong desire to just get away occasionally. Maybe it's time to kindly say those three little words: "Leave me alone!"

—Lyn Cryderman

*R*eflect on what I am saying, for the Lord will give you insight into all this.

—*2 Timothy 2:7*

*I*f I speak in the tongues of men and of angels, but have not love, I am only a resounding gong or a clanging cymbal.

—*1 Corinthians 13:1*

O blessed the house, whate'er befall,
Where Jesus Christ is all in all!
Yea, if He were not dwelling there,
How dark and poor and void it were!
O blessed that house where faith ye find
And all within have set their mind
To trust their God and serve Him still,
And do in all His holy will!

—Author unknown

*M*ales and females just don't think the same way. As we relate to each other there seems to be a translation gap. The problem is that the people involved don't generally know that.

In the sixties and seventies, and even in the early

eighties, we were all taught that the sexes were the same; we were supposed to be unisex. That philosophy didn't last long. In fact, it was an insult to both genders. Each gender comes into marriage with very special, individualized qualities. And we speak different "languages."

Each of us needs to understand what the other means; we need to be "bilingual" in our approach to life. Remember Lindy and John? He didn't have any problem making love after they had been arguing all evening. To Lindy, it was an insult to even suggest that they do something so intimate when they weren't getting along. Each person thought the other had a problem. But the problem was that they weren't allowing for the fact that each of them responded to life differently.

—Dr. Henry Brandt

𝒫raise the LORD. Give thanks to the LORD, for he is good; his love endures forever.

—*Psalm 106:1*

𝒯aste and see that the LORD is good; blessed is the man who takes refuge in him.

—*Psalm 34:8*

Openness

$\mathcal{L}$ove is the greatest gift and the greatest risk. To be completely open with the one whose opinion matters most, requires a deep trust. It's a difficult balance to achieve in marriage, this standing on the precipice of understanding and rejection. That the risk is worth the result in no way makes it easier to be transparent with one another. God knows how we feel. He risked his own Son to reach out and let a world of fallen people into his heart.

$\mathcal{T}$he emotional and mental differences between men and women can become insurmountable obstacles to a lasting, fulfilling relationship when ignored or misunderstood. However, those same differences, when recognized and appreciated, can become stepping-stones to a meaningful, fulfilling relationship.

—Gary Smalley

My purpose is that they may be encouraged in heart and united in love, so that they may have the full riches of complete understanding, in order that they may know the mystery of God, namely, Christ, in whom are hidden all the treasures of wisdom and knowledge.

—*Colossians 2:2-3*

Are you willing to take the risk to grow together in your marriage so the second half is far better than the first half? It may involve making yourself more vulnerable to your spouse and disclosing yourself in a deeper way. Or it may involve re-arranging your schedule, learning skills, or changing some of your personal habits. But if you want to have a more personal and satisfying relationship with your spouse for the second half of marriage, we encourage you to take this challenge seriously.

—David & Claudia Arp

Whoever would love life and see good days must keep … his lips from deceitful speech…. he must seek peace and pursue it.

—*1 Peter 3:10-11*

*L*overs begin to see each other almost as if through the eyes of God. One husband said, "My wife sees a side of me that no one else sees. I feel as though she knows the true me, and her love filters out all the faults that the other people might notice."

—Ed Wheat

*E*veryone lives by a set of rules that is rarely spoken but always known. Needless to say, unspoken rules become more vocal when our spouse "breaks" them.

—Drs. Les & Leslie Parrott

*L*ove must be sincere.

—*Romans 12:9*

*D*o not conform any longer to the pattern of this world, but be transformed by the renewing of your mind. Then you will be able to test and approve what God's will is—his good, pleasing and perfect will.

—*Romans 12:2*

$\mathscr{L}$ove is blind during the cool evenings of
romance, but sees 20/15 (a little better than 20/20)
when the cloudless noonday sun begins to bake.
Shortly into marriage couples discover they do have
different goals, different expectations, and different
values. The very differences that fascinated in the
beginning create friction down the line.
Listen to the words of counselor Paul Tournier:

"When instituting marriage, God declared, 'They
shall no longer be two, but one.' As soon as a couple begin to hide matters from one another they
compromise the basic oneness of marital life."

—Patrick Morley

$\mathscr{J}$esus said,
"But whoever lives by the truth comes into the
light, so that it may be seen plainly that what he
has done has been done through God."

—John 3:21

$\mathscr{G}$od can testify how I long for all of you with
the affection of Christ Jesus. And this is my prayer:
that your love may abound more and more in
knowledge and depth of insight.

—Philippians 1:8–9

*L*ooking back, it seems silly that Les and I did so much to prepare for our wedding and so little to prepare for our marriage. … We never had premarital counseling, but we spent the first year of our married life in therapy. Once a week, we met with a counselor who helped us iron out the wrinkles we never even saw before getting married. Not that we were in serious trouble. But we had this naïve idea that after our wedding our life would fall naturally into place, and a marriage preparation course or counseling never entered our minds.

—Drs. Les & Leslie Parrott

*J*esus said,
"And I will ask the Father, and he will give you another Counselor to be with you forever—the Spirit of truth. The world cannot accept him, because it neither sees him nor knows him. But you know him, for he lives with you and will be in you."

John 14:16–17

"*F*or there is nothing hidden that will not be disclosed, and nothing concealed that will not be known or brought out into the open," Jesus told us.

—*Luke 8:17*

Communication is the way one person opens up to make himself known to another person. It's how a person shares his or her feelings. Today's adult, however, is so afraid of feeling that he or she stays busy and avoids any in-depth involvement. That avoidance includes in-depth communication with a spouse. Hence, these individuals find themselves ten years into a marriage and still very lonely. They discover that their loneliness has nothing to do with their proximity to another person. They may sleep next to their spouse and still be very lonely. The loneliness they are experiencing comes from their lack of in-depth, ongoing communication—the kind of communication that means they are willing to open the door to their heart and risk vulnerability.

The primary reason for communication is not to share facts. Fact-sharing is simply the most basic form of communication. Communication at its best is defined as time spent opening the doors to one another's innermost self. Let me emphasize that by restating it: Communication is a long-term process by which two people talk in such a way as to open themselves up to one another and share who they really are.

—Robert & Rosemary Barnes

Integrity

*I*ntegrity in a marriage is that gut-level, what-you-see-is-what-you-get honesty that builds trust between two people. Where there is integrity, there are no hidden agendas, no skeletons in the closet, no hiding from true emotion, no fear of confrontation.

Instead there is the ability to love unselfishly because love springs from pure hearts. In the place of fear there is confidence that the loved one will always do good and never evil. In place of hiding emotions behind words there is the ability to confront—to put it all out on the table and work through any crisis because each has an abiding faith in each other.

In a marriage, there is no greater betrayal than the betrayal of integrity. Integrity is the groundwork, the core, the foundation upon which the rest of the marriage structure is built. We must guard our hearts so that we never once lose our integrity as individuals or as a couple.

I strive always to keep my conscience clear before God and man.

—Acts 24:16

*W*e are taking pains to do what is right, not only in the eyes of the Lord but also in the eyes of men.

—*2 Corinthians 8:21*

*T*he LORD loves the just and will not forsake his faithful ones.

—*Psalm 37:28*

*W*ho walks righteously and speaks what is right, who rejects gain from extortion and keeps his hand from accepting bribes, who … shuts his eyes against contemplating evil … will dwell on the heights, whose refuge will be the mountain fortress. His bread will be supplied, and water will not fail him.

—*Isaiah 33:15-16*

*P*ray for us. We are sure that we have a clear conscience and desire to live honorably in every way.

—*Hebrews 13:18*

*U*ltimately, to achieve a success that really matters, we each must balance our desire for vocational success against our other priorities.

—*Patrick Morley*

In the heart of every man burns an intense desire to lead a more significant life. A man's most innate need is his need to be significant—to find meaning and purpose to life, to make a difference, to accomplish something with his life.

—Patrick Morley

Respect your feelings, listen to their warnings, but do not let them control you. God has given you a free will and the power to choose. You are in charge.

—Ed Wheat

Learning how to rise above difficult circumstances may be the greatest gift you can give your spouse.

—Drs. Les & Leslie Parrott

When the qualities of courage, persistence, gratefulness, calmness, gentleness, and unselfish love are present in a person's character, it is easier to receive his or her words and to follow his or her instruction or example. This is no less true for your marriage.

—Gary Smalley

*W*hoever sows sparingly will also reap sparingly, and whoever sows generously will also reap generously.

—*2 Corinthians 9:6*

"*S*o in everything, do to others what you would have them do to you, for this sums up the Law and the Prophets," Jesus said.

—*Matthew 7:12*

*T*he best way to get what we need is to practice the foundational rule of civilized societies everywhere: "Do unto others as you would have them do unto you."

—*Patrick Morley*

*P*erhaps the first thing that newlyweds learn is that two can live as cheaply as one—for half as long. Getting lifestyle in line with income is a tough requirement during those first years of marriage…. What one partner finds an absolute necessity, the other views as an unnecessary luxury.

—*Gary Smalley*

The fulfillment of love hinges on closeness, sharing, communication, honesty, and support.

—Drs. Les & Leslie Parrott,

The same way you judge others, you will be judged, and with the measure you use, it will be measured to you. Why do you look at the speck of sawdust in your brother's eye and pay no attention to the plank in your own eye?

—Matthew 7:2-3

Jesus instructed,

"And what does the LORD require of you? To act justly and to love mercy and to walk humbly with your God."

—Micah 6:8

Family values shape our character. Family experiences influence our concepts of how marriage should be structured and how children should be raised, and of how we should view work, recreation, education, money, politics, and religion.

—Bill & Lynne Hybels

$\mathcal{T}$hree viruses in particular infect us with "success sickness": The rat race, leading an unexamined life, and cultural Christianity.

To run the rat race is to endlessly pursue an ever increasing prosperity that ends not in contentment but frustration. To lead an unexamined life means to rush from task to task, but not call enough time-outs to reflect on life's larger meaning and purpose.

Cultural Christianity means to seek the God we want instead of the God who is. It is the tendency to be shallow in our understanding of God, wanting him to be a gentle grandfather who spoils us and lets us have our own way.

—Patrick Morley

$\mathcal{I}$ allow a few other couples to hold me accountable for loving my wife and children. They have the freedom to ask me how we're doing, as a couple and as a family, and I know they love me enough to lift me up when I fall. And I always try to remember that love is a choice. I choose to care about my relationships. That same choice leading to great rewards can be yours.

—Gary Smalley

In a national survey conducted for Promise Keepers, men were asked why they kept their promises. The two answers given most often were *participation in church-based small groups* and *supportive wives.*

—Patrick Morley

Live such good lives among the pagans that, though they accuse you of doing wrong, they may see your good deeds and glorify God on the day he visits us.

—*1 Peter 2:12*

If you really keep the royal law found in Scripture, "Love your neighbor as yourself," you are doing right.

—*James 2:8*

Finally, brothers, whatever is true, whatever is noble, whatever is right, whatever is pure, whatever is lovely, whatever is admirable—if anything is excellent or praiseworthy—think about such things.

—*Philippians 4:8*

*B*etter a poor but wise youth than an old but foolish king who no longer knows how to take warning.

—*Ecclesiastes 4:13*

*I*ntegrity is not something you are born with, but something you·must earn. And keep. All it takes is one wrong move for your reputation to be damaged. Most of us really do know the difference between right and wrong, but it's all too easy to see the good that might come from an unethical choice. Once you begin to rationalize a particular decision that has ethical implications, you need to stop everything and ask yourself, "Am I trying to talk myself into something I know is wrong?"

No one is free of all regrets. You may have made some ethical errors in the past and feel pretty small. Maybe you've been heading in the wrong direction, but in your heart you really want to become a person of character and integrity. You can do it! Commit this day's decisions and activities to God and let Him guide you to a higher standard of honesty.

—Bob Briner

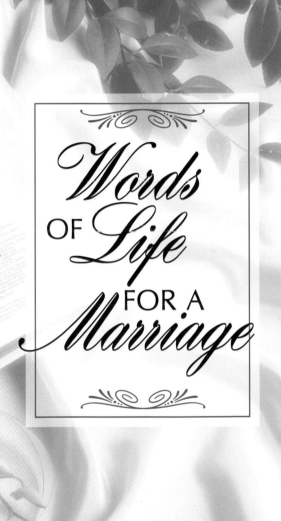

Words
OF *Life*
FOR A
Marriage

*N*o other person can look in through the window of our heart as well as a marriage partner. Our greatest support in achieving our good intentions and growth can come from a life partner. It's not what we say that is important, but what we mean and what we do. Respect is earned in the doing of little things—calling to say you'll be late, remembering to follow through with a promise, giving grace when the other person fails to realize you'll need the favor returned sooner or later. All other grand themes of marriage will follow when first we reach for one another with the grace of forgiveness and humility.

*W*hen Jesus spoke again to the people, he said, "I am the light of the world. Whoever follows me will never walk in darkness, but will have the light of life."

—John 8:12

*T*hough one may be overpowered, two can defend themselves. A cord of three strands is not quickly broken.

—Ecclesiastes 4:12

*Y*our soul's fingers stretch out
   reaching for heaven.
Can you feel its warmth
   standing on tiptoe?

Trembling on the precipice
Touching you, I disappear
   at the edge of time.
I recognize your heart.

—Pat Matuszak

"*T*here are three things that are too amazing
for me, four that I do not understand: the way of
an eagle in the sky, the way of a snake on a rock,
the way of a ship on the high seas, and the way of
a man with a maiden."

—*Proverbs 30:18–19*

*S*aying "I do" brings with it a host of conscious
and unconscious expectations that aren't always
fulfilled.

—Drs. Les & Leslie Parrott,

We stand at the doorway...
   ...saying good-bye
   ...and not going

Filled with words
   ...we cannot spell
A silence that embarrasses us
   ...we of paper eloquence

Now adrift in the void
   ...before the word

Empty space filled with meaning
   ...eluding expression

Space of poetry
   ...an empty doorway

—Pat Matuszak

Jesus said, "I am the true vine, and my Father is the gardener. ...Remain in me, and I will remain in you. No branch can bear fruit by itself; it must remain in the vine. Neither can you bear fruit unless you remain in me. I am the vine; you are the branches. If a man remains in me and I in him, he will bear much fruit; apart from me you can do nothing. If anyone does not remain in me, he is like a branch that is thrown away and withers."

—*John 15:1, 4–6*

*M*y heart is like a singing bird
    Whose nest is in a watered shoot;
My heart is like an apple tree
    Whose boughs are bent with thickset fruit;
My heart is like a rainbow shell
    That paddles in a halcyon sea;
My heart is gladder than all these
    Because by love is come to me.

—Christian Rossetti

*P*eople who have successfully built an intimate relationship know its power and comfort, but they also know that taking the emotional risks that allow intimacy to happen isn't easy.

—Drs. Les & Leslie Parrott

*N*ow to him who is able to do immeasurably more than all we ask or imagine, according to his power that is at work within us, to him be glory . . .

—*Ephesians 3:20-21*

"I'm sorry."

*I*f a husband and wife can understand how to maintain harmony by immediately working to clear up every hurtful offense between them, they can climb out of such common problems and even marriage's deepest pit—divorce.

—Gary Smalley

*D*o not let any unwholesome talk come out of your mouths, but only what is helpful for building others up according to their needs, that it may benefit those who listen. And do not grieve the Holy Spirit of God.

—*Ephesians 4:29-30*

A gentle answer turns away wrath, but a harsh word stirs up anger.

—*Proverbs 15:1*

$\mathscr{O}$f all the holy acts that go against our grain as fallen humans, the strongest may well be admitting we are wrong, that we need forgiveness, whether from God or our spouse. Yet no other act is so powerful in coming to terms honestly with our sin. Admitting to wrong calls down the mercy of Christ from the very throne of grace. This action restores our heart in love. Admission of wrongdoing sets us free to give and receive love when we unlock the door, fling it open unconditionally to God and others.

Bargaining with God is not possible. We must surrender ourselves to Him unconditionally. Give Him everything. He will give you back far more.

—Georges Bernanos

$\mathscr{M}$arriage is, in actual fact, just a way of living. Before marriage, we don't expect life to be all sunshine and roses, but we seem to expect marriage to be that way.

—Drs. Les & Leslie Parrott

*T*here are many times we let each other down—like when Dave doesn't keep up with the time and is late again or when Claudia falls asleep when Dave has planned a romantic evening for us. It's times like these when we look to our faith in God to keep our cord strong. In our marriage, we like to think about Dave being one strand, Claudia being one strand, and God's Holy Spirit being the third strand that holds it all together when our individual strands are frayed.

—David & Claudia Arp

*B*e imitators of God, therefore, as dearly loved children and live a life of love, just as Christ loved us and gave himself up for us as a fragrant offering and sacrifice to God.

—Ephesians 5:1-2

*W*hen we were still powerless, Christ died for the ungodly. Very rarely will anyone die for a righteous man. . . . But God demonstrates his own love for us in this: While we were still sinners, Christ died for us.

—Romans 5:6-8

"Ask and it will be given to you; seek and you will find; knock and the door will be opened to you. For everyone who asks receives; he who seeks finds; and to him who knocks, the door will be opened." Jesus encouraged us.

—Matthew 7:7-8

When we have been offended by someone, we usually don't want to hear a glib "I'm sorry." We want to know that the person realizes he or she was wrong and that he or she hurt us. I believe there are a lot of "wrong ways" to ask forgiveness. They are wrong because they do not bring us into harmony with the person whom we have offended and they may not communicate the person's value to us.

—Gary Smalley

All relationships are difficult, especially marriage. I once heard Florence Littauer say, "We are attracted to marry each other's strengths, and then go home to live with each other's weaknesses."

—Patrick Morley

*U*se anger and conflict in a creative way to build your relationship. Love and anger can both be used to build your marriage, but you must process your anger in an appropriate way and develop a proper balance that allows you to express your concerns in the context of a loving relationship. A healthy marriage is a safe place to resolve honest conflict and process anger. The reason this challenge is so critical to long-term marriages is that in most conflict situations, it isn't the facts that are the real problem, it's the strong negative (or even angry) feelings we harbor. Once those feelings are dealt with, it's simple to move on and work at resolving the conflict.

—David & Claudia Arp

*F*inally, all of you, live in harmony with one another; be sympathetic, … be compassionate and humble.

—*1 Peter 3:8*

A humble admission of wrong produces positive results.

—Gary Smalley

*H*umility comes before honor.

—*Proverbs 15:33*

*W*hen my heart was grieved and my spirit embittered, I was senseless and ignorant; I was a brute beast before you. Yet I am always with you; you hold me by my right hand. You guide me with your counsel, and afterward you will take me into glory. Whom have I in heaven but you? And earth has nothing I desire besides you. My flesh and my heart may fail, but God is the strength of my heart and my portion forever.

—*Psalm 73:21–26*

*O*ur job is to choose to love each other. It's not a feeling. It's not even passion. Love is a choice that we make. It's an action that we choose to take toward that person we are loving. You aren't *in* love; you do love.

—Robert & Rosemary Barnes

"I forgive you."

*L*ove is patient, love is kind. It does not envy, it does not boast, it is not proud. It is not rude, it is not self-seeking, it is not easily angered, it keeps no record of wrongs.

—*1 Corinthians 13:4-5*

*F*orgiveness is a key element in healthy, long-term marriages. Forgiveness is the oil that lubricates a love relationship, and it's an oil we need daily. Forgiveness is not a one-time event; it's an attitude of wanting to partner with your spouse in spite of his or her imperfections and irritations.
We suggested two important steps [for forgiveness]:
1. Decide to forgive.
2. Don't put a limit on forgiveness.

—*David & Claudia Arp,*

*B*e merciful, just as your Father is merciful.

—*Luke 6:36*

*B*lessed are the merciful, for they will be shown mercy.

—Matthew 5:7

*A*ll marriages need forgiveness and a big dose of reality. No spouse is perfect! Even when we are trying to please the other, we can mess up. … Do you have a squeaky marriage that needs the oil of forgiveness? We do.

—David & Claudia Arp

*A*nd when you stand praying, if you hold anything against anyone, forgive him, so that your Father in heaven may forgive you your sins.

—Mark 11:25

*D*uring times of testing and disappointments, we kept working on our relationship. We learned how to forgive each other and how to work things out. We are committed to our marriage and we never give up. That's our secret.

—Wife married forty years

*M*arriage becomes a series of surprises for most of us, and one of them is how frequently we need to forgive and be forgiven. ... Even the best relationship cannot remain intact for long without forgiveness.

—Ed Wheat

*G*entleness is showing tender consideration for the feelings of another. ... The key motivation for gentleness is maintaining an awareness of the extreme fragility of other people's feelings.

—Gary Smalley

*A*nd hope does not disappoint us, because God has poured out his love into our hearts by the Holy Spirit, whom he has given us.

—*Romans 5:5*

*B*e kind and compassionate to one another, forgiving each other, just as in Christ God forgave you.

—*Ephesians 4:32*

A heart at peace gives life to the body.

—*Proverbs 14:30*

A man's wisdom gives him patience; it is to his glory to overlook an offense.

—*Proverbs 19:11*

O ur relationship with God empowers us to forgive each other and to be willing to say, "I'm sorry. Will you please forgive me?" No human relationship offers the closeness and intimacy of the marriage relationship, but with it also comes the greatest opportunity for anger and conflict. So along with our faith in God comes our determination to learn how to cope with anger and make our marriage work.

—David & Claudia Arp

M ake every effort to keep the unity of the Spirit through the bond of peace.

—*Ephesians 4:3*

*W*hen someone has wronged us and said, "I'm sorry" we want to "forgive and forget"—but it's just not always that simple. Real forgiveness involves more than stuffing down our hurt feelings and trying to forget. When we stuff a hurt feeling it is just under the surface, ready to resurrect again. Jesus came to set us free, to heal our sorrows so that we can truly forgive. Then instead of merely forgetting, we understand.

The most humble of human beings, even when he thinks he can no longer love, retains within his soul the power of love. We are not the ones who invented love. Love follows its own order, its own rules. God himself is love . … If love is your desire, don't flee beyond love's reach.

—Georges Bernanos

*T*o form a forever relationship, you will need a *love-centered* marriage. … God of Love has made His own love available to each of us. That love, which the Bible calls *agape*, never changes. It is unconditional and does not depend on a person's behavior. It goes right on showing kindness to the beloved, no matter what, because it is controlled not by our emotions, but by our will. The ability to love this way is a gift from God through His Son Jesus Christ; His love channeled through us blesses our mate and our marriage.

—Ed Wheat

*J*esus replied, "If anyone loves me, he will obey my teaching. My Father will love him, and we will come to him and make our home with him. He who does not love me will not obey my teaching. These words you hear are not my own; they belong to the Father who sent me. All this I have spoken while still with you. But the Counselor, the Holy Spirit, whom the Father will send in my name, will teach you all things and will remind you of everything I have said to you. Peace I leave with you; my peace I give you. I do not give to you as the world gives. Do not let your hearts be troubled and do not be afraid."

—John 14:23–27

*I*f you, O LORD, kept a record of sins, O Lord, who could stand? But with you there is forgiveness.

—Psalm 130:3-4

*G*etting married cannot instantly cure all our ills, but marriage *can* become a powerful healing agent over time. If you are patient, marriage can help you overcome even some of the toughest of tribulations.

—Drs. Les & Leslie Parrott

I have waited for you here
    always
    in this fixed place
    separate from
all the world

A feeling I have always been here
    that we were always here together and will
remain forever

A sad smile, yet joyful,
    our eyes glistening, faces wet with tears
    of love, of loss, the kinds that heal

We meet forever next to the fountain of the blind
    and see our reflection in a circle of pure
    gold.

—Pat Matuszak

I slept but my heart was awake.
  Listen! My lover is knocking:
"Open to me, my sister, my darling,
  my dove, my flawless one.
My head is drenched with dew,
  my hair with the dampness of the night."
. . . My lover thrusts his hand through the latch-
opening;
  my heart began to pound for him,
I arose to open for my lover,
  and my hands dripped with myrrh,
on the handles of the lock.
  I opened for my lover,
but my lover had left; he was gone.
  My heart sank at his departure.
I looked for him but did not find him.
  I called for him but he did not answer . . .
If you find my lover,
  what will you tell him?
Tell him I am faint with love.

—*Song of Songs 5:2–6,8*

"I love you."

It's a huge step in any relationship when we realize we are in love. Three words— "I love you"—take us across the threshold of our lives as separate souls into the realm of being a couple. After saying these words, all our other words begin to change. It becomes "us" instead of "I" and "we" instead of "me" in all our thoughts and plans. But it's not enough to remember that we once said them for the first time. No, we must go on finding reasons to say "I love you" again and again. Then we find other words that mean our love is still growing and that we haven't forgotten. And sometimes we find other ways to communicate love without words and sometimes without even realizing we are speaking more than a sonnet could by our actions.

In the hiding places on the mountainside, show me your face, let me hear your voice; for your voice is sweet.

—*Song of Songs 2:14*

Most couples start with love. But who can say how love really begins? Each of you has a different story to tell, for romantic love takes surprising turns in its development.

—*Ed Wheat*

When asked, "What makes a good marriage?" the answer given by nearly 90 percent of the population is "Being in love." When asked to list the essential ingredients of love as a basis for marriage, however, a survey of more than a thousand college students revealed that "no single item was mentioned by at least one-half of those responding." In other words, we can't agree on what love is. … As one person in the survey said, "Love is like lightning—you may not know what it is, but you do know when it hits you."

—*Drs. Les & Leslie Parrott*

*E*very husband and every wife is different and has different ways of giving and receiving love. ...For some people touch is the primary language of love. Their spouse can say "I love you" twenty times a day... but without an embrace or a kiss or a squeeze they won't feel loved. Other people need to hear verbal expressions of love. They need to hear in concrete terms why their spouse loves them. ... Service is what makes some people feel most loved. They respond best to affection that is revealed in practical terms. ... Gifts make other people feel loved—not because of the cost involved, but because of the personal attention and thought that goes into them.... Spending time together makes other people feel loved. They don't care particularly what they and their spouses do, as long as they are together.

—Bill & Lynne Hybels

*M*ake many acts of love, for they set the soul on fire and make it gentle. Whatever thou doest, offer it up to God, and pray it may be for his honor and glory.

—St. Teresa of Avila

$\mathcal{T}$he more we take others for granted, the less gentle we tend to be in our relationship with them. We lose sight of their precious value and fragile inner person.

In other words, "The more we value something, the more gentle we will be in handling it." If I handed you a three-thousand-year-old, paper-thin Oriental vase worth $50,000 and asked you to take it to the bank, would you handle it differently than if I gave you a fifty-nine-cent plastic vase and asked you to take it down the street?

—Gary Smalley

$\mathcal{A}$ttraction is an emotion that ebbs and flows. Only if attraction grows into a genuine love does it become steady and stable enough to build a marriage on.

—Bill & Lynne Hybels

$\mathcal{B}$oth partners in a marriage desire and need physical intimacy, which includes both *sexual intimacy* and *nonsexual* touching.

—Patrick Morley

Come live with me, and be my love,

And we will all the pleasures prove,

That valleys, groves, hills and fields,

Woods, or steepy mountains yields.

And we will sit upon the rocks,

seeing the shepherds feed their flocks, By

shallow rivers, to whose falls,

Melodious birds sing madrigals.

And I will make the beds of roses,

And a thousand fragrant posies,

A cap of lowers, and a kirtle

Embroidered all with leaves o myrtle'

A gown made of the finest wool,

Which from our pretty lambs we pull,

Fair-lined slippers for the cold,

With buckles of the purest gold;

A belt of straw and ivy buds

With coral clasps and amber studs;

And if these pleasures may thee move,

Come live with me, and be my love.

The shepherd swains shall dance and sing,

For thy delight each May morning;

If these delights thy mind may move,

Then live with me, and be my love.

—Christopher Marlowe

*H*ow beautiful your sandaled feet, O prince's daughter! Your graceful legs are like jewels, the work of a craftsman's hands.

How beautiful you are and how pleasing, O love, with your delights!

I belong to my lover, and his desire is for me.

Come, my lover, let us go to the countryside, let us spend the night in the villages.

Let us go early to the vineyards to see if the vines have budded, if their blossoms have opened, and if the pomegranates are in bloom — there I will give you my love.

The mandrakes send out their fragrance, and at our door is every delicacy, both new and old, that I have stored up for you, my lover.

—*Song of Songs 7:1,6,10–13*

*O*ne woman in her mid-fifties said she enjoys a card or flowers from her husband because they separate her from her identity with her home and family. The gift singles her out as an individual with an individual's identity and self-worth.

—*Gary Smalley*

$\mathcal{L}$earn to express your feelings through three loving attitudes: warmth, empathy, and sincerity.

Warmth is the friendly acceptance of a person.

Empathy is the ability to understand and identify with a person's feelings.

Sincerity is showing a genuine concern for a person without changing your attitude toward him when circumstances change.

—Gary Smalley

Clinging TO THE *One You Love*

*S*ome days it's easy to cling to your spouse. Things are running smoothly. You've had a great conversation and seem to have reached real understanding of each other. You feel valued and cared for. It's like picking apples in a morning garden with the fresh, sweet dew of love that seems to linger on your relationship because of special moments and words. But other days life together seems down and ordinary, more like applesauce than a walk through an orchard. Those are the times when love is a decision. Holding on to your commitment then can cause love to deepen and blossom into more than a fickle string of emotional moments. Commitment is the way to build a love that will last forever.

*W*hat do you say when an unmarried person asks "How did you know this was the one?" Maybe you didn't! Maybe it took some time. Did your spouse just keep showing up until you "grew accustomed" to that one's familiar face? Did you wake up one day and realize your life would be a pretty gray place without this person? Or did you have one of those love at first sight romances? (A magic hat trick meeting that completely pulled the tablecloth out from under your carefully set agenda!) There are so many combinations of circumstances for everyone who falls in love. How can you answer about knowing this was the one? Whatever route you took, you finally ended up at the place where you knew in a way that spoke to your heart.

—Anonymous

A longing fulfilled is sweet to the soul.

—*Proverbs 13:19*

*E*very man reaches a point at which he craves someone with whom to share his life.

—Patrick Morley

*A*rise, my darling; my beautiful one and, come with me. See! The winter is past; the rains are over and gone. Flowers appear on the earth; the season of singing has come.

—*Song of Songs 2:10-12*

*M*arriage is a mysterious, spiritual fusion of two distinct lives into one flesh. What was the man before woman was taken from his body? Alone and needing help. The creation of woman and marriage was always anticipated by our omniscient Creator.

—Patrick Morley

*L*ove is a movement, effusion, and advancement of the heart toward the good. The soul cannot live without love.

—St. Francis de Sales

*M*y people will live in peaceful dwelling places, in secure homes, in undisturbed places of rest.

—*Isaiah 32:18*

*T*he husband should fulfill his marital duty to his wife, and likewise the wife to her husband. The wife's body does not belong to her alone but also to her husband. In the same way, the husband's body does not belong to him alone but also to his wife. Do not deprive each other.

—1 Corinthians 7:3-5

*T*wo people falling in love is a powerful emotional event. That it happens to both lovers at the same time intensifies the sense of delight. There is the thrill of newness and a sense of wonder as if the two lovers have entered into a new reality.

—Ed Wheat

*H*e will be called Wonderful Counselor, Mighty God, Everlasting Father, Prince of Peace. Of the increase of his government and peace there will be no end. He will reign on David's throne and over his kingdom, establishing and upholding it with justice and righteousness from that time on and forever. The zeal of the Lord Almighty will accomplish this.

—Isaiah 9:6–7

On Meeting You

$\mathcal{T}$he darkness dissolved that day
    into a dew-drenched world
    of no impossibility.

There I awoke and put down roots
    Unfurled leaves—mine, green, and shining
    with the dew of that dawn.

And you, all gray-plumed, nested in my branches
    as was the way of winged creatures
    with rooted ones.

As your wing cut the liquid depth of that reality
    I trembled at your touch—the breach of air
    made by your passing.

Light filtered through my leaves
    Your silent gray began to sing—but only I
       could hear it
    all other words were silence to me,
    all other colors gray
    beside the riot of shades
    you had become.

—Pat Matuszak

$\mathcal{H}$is banner over me is love.

—Song of Songs 2:4

$\mathscr{P}$raise the LORD, O my soul, and forget not all his benefits—who forgives all your sins and heals all your diseases, who redeems your life from the pit and crowns you with love and compassion, who satisfies your desires with good things so that your youth is renewed like the eagle's.

—*Psalm 103:2-5*

$\mathscr{D}$elight yourself in the LORD and he will give you the desires of your heart.

—*Psalm 37.4*

$\mathscr{Y}$our inner self, the unfading beauty of a gentle and quiet spirit, ... is of great worth in God's sight.

—*1 Peter 3:4*

$\mathscr{H}$eaven's resources. They are truths you can count upon concerning God's readiness to help you build the kind of marriage you dream of now. ... It is God's will in every marriage that the couple love each other with an absorbing spiritual, emotional, and physical attraction that continues to grow throughout their lifetime together.

—*Ed Wheat*

As high as the heavens are above the earth, so great is [God's] love.

—*Psalm 103:11*

Genuine love doesn't necessarily spring from feelings. Its basis is primarily a concern for the welfare of another. Although the feelings of affection will follow, genuine love is initially an action directed toward fulfilling another person's needs.

—Gary Smalley

The success of a marriage comes not in finding the "right" person, but in the ability of both partners to adjust to the real person they inevitably realize they married.

— John Fisher

When love and skill work together, expect a masterpiece.

—John Ruskin

Happiness seems made to be shared.

—Corneille

The Good-morrow

I wonder by my troth, what thou and I
Did, till we lov'd? were we not wean'd till then?
But suck'd on country pleasures, childishly?
Or snorted we in the seven sleepers' den?
'Twas so; but this, all pleasures fancies be.
If ever any beauty I did see,
Which I desir'd, and got, 'twas but a dream of
thee.

An now good-morrow to our waking souls,
Which watch not one another out of fear;
For love all love of other sights controls,
And makes one little room in everywhere.
Let sea-discovers to new worlds have gone,
Let maps to other, worlds, on worlds have shown,
Let us possess one world, each hath one, and is one.

My face in thine eye, thine in mine appears,
And true plain hearts do in the faces rest;
Where can we find two better hemispheres
Without sharp North, with declining west?

What ever dies, was not mixt equally;
If our two loves be one, or thou and I
Love so alike that none do slacken, none can die.

—John Donne

*L*ove is a great thing,
A great good in every way; it alone
lightens what is heavy, and leads
smoothly over all roughness, for it carries
a burden without being burdened, and
makes every bitter thing sweet and tasty....

Nothing is sweeter than love,
nothing higher, nothing fuller,
nothing better in heaven and earth....

—Thomas à Kempis

*Y*ou are forgiving and good, O LORD, abound-
ing in love to all who call to you.

—*Psalm 86:5*

*L*ive as children of light.

—*Ephesians 5:8*

*L*ove is like a tennis match; you'll never win
consistently until you learn to serve well.

—Dan P. Herod

*L*ast summer we went with a close friend to his ranch in Jackson Hole, Wyoming. At our friend Gary's insistence, we spent one whole day climbing the side of a mountain to get to something he wanted us to see. We were both just exhausted, and it got to the point that we really didn't care what was in that special valley. It couldn't be worth all that pain we were going through. He just kept insisting. "Trust me," he kept saying, "you'll be glad you did this when we get there."

Three hours later, when our feet were blistered and we were dying of thirst, we finally reached our destination. Lying down on a side of a mountain, we were looking at the most beautiful valley and lake I had ever seen. The climb was long and it was agony, but it was more than worth it.

In the beginning, God established marriage. It wasn't meant to be easy; nothing worth having is. It was meant to be fulfilling and completing. It takes work, but it's almost as if God is saying, "Trust Me, it's worth the effort!"

—Robert & Rosemary Barnes

Forsaking All Others, PUTTING YOUR MARRIAGE FIRST

*L*et love and faithfulness never leave you; bind them around your neck, write them on the tablet of your heart. Then you will win favor and a good name in the sight of God and man.

—*Proverbs 3:3-4*

"*F*or this reason a man will leave his father and mother and be united to his wife, and the two will become one flesh." This is a profound mystery—but I am talking about Christ and the church. However, each one of you also must love his wife as he loves himself, and the wife must respect her husband.

—*Ephesians 5:31-33*

*L*overs long to be together. … This happens because they have become bonded emotionally and now crave that feeling of security and at-homeness, which they find only in the other's presence.

—Ed Wheat

*M*ay the Lord direct your hearts into God's love and Christ's perseverance.

—*2 Thessalonians 3:5*

*T*he grace of God that brings salvation has appeared to all men. It teaches us to say "No" to ungodliness and worldly passions, and to live self-controlled, upright and godly lives in this present age.

—*Titus 2:11-12*

*N*o temptation has seized you except what is common to man. And God is faithful; he will not let you be tempted beyond what you can bear. But when you are tempted, he will also provide a way out so that you can stand up under it.

—*1 Corinthians 10:13*

*M*arriage should be honored by all, and the marriage bed kept pure, for God will judge the adulterer and all the sexually immoral.

—*Hebrews 13:4*

*S*o guard yourself in your spirit, and do not break faith with the wife of your youth.

—*Malachi 2:15*

*F*or this very reason, make every effort to add to your faith goodness; and to goodness, knowledge; and to knowledge, self-control; and to self-control, perseverance; and to perseverance, godliness; and to godliness, brotherly kindness; and to brotherly kindness, love. For if you possess these qualities in increasing measure, they will keep you from being ineffective and unproductive in your knowledge of our Lord Jesus Christ.

—*2 Peter 1:5-8*

*M*ay your fountain be blessed, and may you rejoice in the wife of your youth.

—*Proverbs 5:18*

*F*or the eyes of the LORD range throughout the earth to strengthen those whose hearts are fully committed to him.

—2 Chronicles 16:9

*T*he more you do to build a valuable, healthy relationship, the better you'll feel about your marriage. If you change any of your activities because you want to enrich your relationship, at first you may feel you're giving up your favorite pastime. But in the long run, you'll not only gain a better marriage, but a greater freedom to enjoy other areas of life.

—Gary Smalley

*F*aithfulness is like a multifaceted jewel, exhibiting a complex combination of interrelated dimension—trust, commitment, truth, loyalty, valuing, care. But our faithfulness to each other can only be sustained by God's model of faithfulness to us. When a man and woman covenant with one another, God promises faithfulness to them. And that helps couples keep the faith.

—Drs. Les & Leslie Parrott

*L*et him kiss me with the kisses of his
mouth — for your love is more delightful
   than wine.
Pleasing is the fragrance of your perfumes;
   your name is like perfume poured out.
   No wonder the maidens love you!
Take me away with you —let us hurry! Let
   the king bring me into his chambers. We
   rejoice and delight in you; we will
   praise your love more than wine.
How right they are to adore you!
   Dark am I, yet lovely, O daughters of
Jerusalem, dark like the tents of Kedar, like
   the tent curtains of Solomon.

How beautiful you are, my darling! Oh, how
    beautiful! Your eyes are doves.
How handsome you are, my lover! Oh, how
    charming! And our bed is verdant.
The beams of our house are cedars; our
    rafters are firs.
I am a rose of Sharon, a lily of the valleys.
    Like a lily among thorns is my darling
    among the maidens.
Like an apple tree among the trees of the
    forest is my lover among the young men.
I delight to sit in his shade, and his fruit is
sweet to my taste.

Song of Songs 1:2–5, 15–17, 2:1–3

*M*y love has placed her little hand
    With noble faith in mine,
And vowed that wedlock's sacred band
    Our natures shall entwine.
My love has sworn, with sealing kiss,
    With me to live—to die;
I have at last my nameless bliss:
    As I love—loved am I!

                 —Charlotte Brontë

*B*ut you are a shield around me, O LORD.

                 —Psalm 3:3

*S*hall I compare thee to a summer's day?
Thou art more lovely and more temperate.
Rough winds do shake the darling buds of May,

And summer's lease hath all too short a date.
Sometime too hot the eye of heaven shines,
And often is his gold complexion dimmed;
And every fair from fair sometime declines,
By chance, or nature's changing course,
untrimmed;
But thy eternal summer shall not fade
Nor lose possession of that fair thou ow'st,

Nor shall Death brag thou wand'rest in his shade
When in eternal lines to time thou grow'st.
So long as men can breathe or eyes can see,
So long lives this, and this gives life to thee.

—William Shakespeare

As fair thou art, my bonnie lass,
So deep in love am I:
And I will love thee still, my dear,
Till a' the seas gang dry.

—Robert Burns

The glue of marriage is spiritual harmony, but
we have failed to teach couples how to achieve
what I call "soul harmony" in marriage. For
example, the biggest barrier keeping husbands
and wives from bonding spiritually is that there is
not a bottom-line honesty between them. A couple won't have the significant Bible study and
prayer that is necessary for spiritual bonding
unless they have a commitment to total sharing
and the grace that it takes.

—Charlie W. Shedd

MY
Best Friend

What Best Friends Do

*B*lessed is the one who marries a best friend. After years and years together, the ultimate compliment silver-haired lovers smile upon each other is: "We are best friends." We may no longer play the same sports or enjoy the same hobbies, but we do delight in each other's company. We love being able to call across the house and know that special person is there—that we can be ourselves and not have to make any kind of impression because our partner accepts us for who we are as a whole, not by bits and pieces. We can fight or be apathetic. We can sit together without having to make conversation. We can listen to each other without needing any special point to our talking. We can sing or dance together when we have no ear or sense of rhythm—and even make up our own words if we forget the right ones! That's friendship, that's love—that's life's gift to the soul.

*Y*ou too are being built together to become a dwelling in which God lives by his Spirit.

—*Ephesians 2:22*

*S*uccessful couples are able to find a proper balance between intimacy and autonomy, and this is critical for healthy relationships in the second half of marriage.

—David & Claudia Arp

*E*ven at times when love was questioned, commitment wasn't! We chose to forgive each other, and the result is a marriage of total trust, faith, and of an ever-deepening love and appreciation for my partner.

—Wife married for twenty-five years

A true friend unbosoms freely, advises justly, assists readily, adventures boldly, takes all patiently, defends courageously and continues a friend unchangeably.

—William Penn

*L*ove does not consist in gazing at each other, but in looking together in the same direction.

—Antoine De Saint-Exupéry

*H*ow are we different? You'll always find exceptions to the rule, but research and experience consistently point to a fundamental and powerful distinction between the sexes: Men focus on achievement, women focus on relationships. It sounds overly simplistic, and it probably is. But remembering this general rule can save every couple wear and tear on their marriage and strengthen their bond.

—Drs. Les & Leslie Parrott

*F*aithfulness in marriage means firmly adhering to the commitment you have made. This loving loyalty has two requirements. First, a faithful couple must never allow a third person to intrude into their love relationship. The second requirement for faithfulness involves loving your partner in ways that meet his or her needs and deepest desires.

—Ed Wheat

*T*hose who walk uprightly enter into peace.

—*Isaiah 57:2*

I will sing of your love and justice; to you, O LORD, I will sing praise. I will be careful to lead a blameless life — when will you come to me? I will walk in my house with blameless heart.

—*Psalm 101:1–2*

*Y*our willingness to accept the differences between you will allow you to complement one another in ways that make life better for each of you.

—*C. W. Neal*

*L*overs desire to commit themselves to one another. … Commitment not only demonstrates the quality of their love but attempts to preserve it … forever.

—*Ed Wheat*

*T*he LORD is God. It is he who made us, and we are his.

—*Psalm 100:3*

*S*ee, I have engraved you on the palms of my hands; your walls are ever before me.

—*Isaiah 49:16*

*D*ear children, let us not love with words or tongue but with actions and in truth. This then is how we set our hearts at rest in his presence.

—*1 John 3:18-19*

*I*t is rare to see a life prescheduled to only 80 percent, leaving a margin for responding to the unexpected that God sends our way. ... An NBC Lifestyle Survey reported on March 9, 1995, found that 59 percent of people said they were "very busy but content" and 10 percent said they were "overloaded." Combined, two out of three people report themselves very busy or overloaded.

—Patrick Morley

*K*eep in mind how different you and your partner are—not just your backgrounds, but your emotional make-up. Learn what really matters to your partner, learn his or her emotional language of love, and then act accordingly.

—Ed Wheat

*W*hat do you throw overboard first when you come under pressure? For most of us it's our quiet time, our wives, and our kids. Why is it that we tend to give so much of our time to those who care about us so little, and so little of our time to those people who care about us so much?

—Patrick Morley

I will listen to what God the LORD will say; he promises peace to his people.

—*Psalm 85:8*

*W*here morning dawns and evening fades you call forth songs of joy.

—*Psalm 65:8*

*S*omeone once defined love as "friendship that has caught fire."

—Bill & Lynne Hybels

*T*his is my lover, this my friend.

—*Song of Songs 5:16*

*W*hen wives befriend, encourage, help, respect, and support their husbands they take a huge step toward inoculating their marriages against death by broken heart.

It is true that more men are developing strong male friendships through accountability groups, but even then there remains a certain guardedness. As Oswald Chambers said, "What is the sign of a friend? That he tells you secret sorrows? No, that he tells you secret joys. Many will confide to you their secret sorrows, but the last mark of intimacy is to confide secret joys."

—Patrick Morley

*A*ll intimacies are based on differences.

—Henry James

*M*ysterious is the fusion of two living spirits:
each takes the best from the other, but only to
give it back again enriched with love.

—Romain Rolland

*I*nstead of talking for itself, genuine love gives
to others. It motivates us to help others reach their
full potential in life.

—Gary Smalley

*F*aith is unutterable trust in God, trust which
never dreams that He will not stand by us.

—Oswald Chambers

*I*ntimacy has a "best friend" or "soul mate"
quality about it. We all want someone who
knows us better than anyone else—and still
accepts us. And we want someone who holds
nothing back from us, someone who trusts us
with personal secrets. Intimacy fills our heart's
deepest longings for closeness and acceptance.

—Drs. Les & Leslie Parrott

*L*et me not to the marriage of true minds
Admit impediments, love is not love
Which alters when it alteration finds,
Or bends with the remover to remove.
O no, it is an ever-fixed mark
That looks on tempests and is never shaken;
It is that star to every wand'ring bark,
Whose worth's unknown, although his height
be taken.
Love's not Time's fool, though rosy lips and
cheeks
Within his bending sickle's compass come,
Love alters not with his brief hours and
weeks,
But bears it out even to the edge of doom;
If this be error and upon me proved,
I never writ, nor no man ever loved.

—William Shakespeare

$\mathscr{I}$shot an arrow into the air,
It fell to earth, I knew not where;
For, so swiftly it flew, the sight
Could not follow it in its flight.

I breathed a song into the air,
It fell to earth I knew not where;
For who has sight so keen and strong,
That it can follow the flight of song?

Long, long afterward, in an oak
I found the arrow, still unbroke;
And the song, from beginning to end,
I found again in the heart of a friend.

—Henry Wadsworth Longfellow

$\mathscr{I}$want to be your friend
Forever and ever without break or decay.
When the hills are all flat
And the rivers are all dry,
When it lightens and thunders in winter,
When it rains and snows in summer,
When Heaven and Earth mingle—
Not till then will I part from you.

—Anonymous, China 1st Century

What Best Friends Don't

*B*est friends don't leave when the going gets tough or look to blame you for hard times. They stick by you and give you the kind of encouragement that comes from not only knowing you well, but loving you anyway. They don't give up when things look impossible. They don't look at problems as if it were too much trouble to help again and again. They hold you accountable without mugging you emotionally. They don't even mind if you tell the same story you've told them before, because they like to see you laugh.

*L*ove can be angry...with a kind of anger in which there is no gall, like the dove's and not the raven's.

—Augustine

The old saying "opposites attract" is based on the phenomenon that many individuals are drawn to people who complement them—who are good at things they are not, who complete them in some way.

—Drs. Les & Leslie Parrott,

Unity in marriage is wonderful when it happens, but it's often difficult to achieve. The secret to unity? Years of living together. Years of taking into consideration the other person's needs, feelings, and desires. Years of putting aside your selfish ambitions to nurture your spouse. Years of pursuing common goals. Years of working through differences of opinion to reach a common, satisfactory resolution. Finding unity isn't easy, but it's worth it, for from it comes tremendous strength to bless a family and a world.

The key to becoming one lies in Jesus' prayer to his Father for all believers: "That they may be one as we are one: I in them and you in me."

Do you willingly pledge yourself to put Jesus' plans and priorities first, making them your own? Then you have allowed Jesus to be "in" you.

—Edith Bajema

To love is to give one's time. We never give the impression that we care when we are in a hurry.

—Paul Tournier

God has called us to live in peace.

—1 Corinthians 7:15

Confess your sins to each other and pray for each other so that you may be healed.

—James 5:16

A well-thought-out division of labor is a beautiful thing to watch, whether it's an athletic team, a business, a family, or a marriage—especially if everybody appreciates the contributions of the others. The best marriages have an "agreed upon" division of labor. They don't just "let it happen."

—Patrick Morley

Jesus said,

"For where two or three come together in my name, there am I with them."

—Matthew 18:20

*W*e want to be best friends and close companions.

We want to have a positive outlook on life.

We want to have plans for the future, and as much as we don't like to think about one of us dying, we want to live a fulfilling life even if one of us is left alone without the other.

We want to continue to grow intellectually and be interesting people.

We want to enjoy our family while realizing we can't be the center of their lives.

—David & Claudia Arp

I thank God every time I remember you.

—*Philippians 1:3*

*B*e imitators of God, therefore, as dearly loved children and live a life full of love, just as Christ loved us and gave himself up for us as a fragrant offering and sacrifice to God.

—*Ephesians 5:1–2*

*B*lessed are the peacemakers, for they will be called sons of God.

—*Matthew 5:9*

A happy heart makes the face cheerful, but heartache crushes the spirit.

—*Proverbs 15:13*

*I*t means so much to have a friend
whose love is sure and true . . .
whose encouragement lets us be
the best that we can be, and whose smile brings feelings
of warmth and acceptance.

The Springtime of friendship
blossoms in the light, bright sunshine
of new beginnings and fresh discoveries . . .
like a first-budded flower, the blessing of new friendship
adds a special pleasure to each day . . .

In stories shared and caring ways and under-standing smiles.
Friendship's confidence, like a graceful vine,
keeps two hearts together.

—Beth Swanson

$\mathcal{D}$o not cast me away when I am old; do not forsake me when my strength is gone.

—*Psalm 71:9*

$\mathcal{B}$ut thanks be to God! He gives us the victory through our Lord Jesus Christ.

—*1 Corinthians 15:57*

$\mathcal{B}$ut we have this treasure in jars of clay to show that this all-surpassing power is from God and not from us.

—*2 Corinthians 4:7*

$\mathcal{I}$t takes guts to stay married. … There will be many crises between the wedding day and the golden anniversary, and the people who make it are heroes.

—Howard Whiteman

Partners IN Christ

The dictionary defines a partner as "one who has a share with another ... is a participant ... a partaker ... who shares the profits and risks." A partner is also defined as "either of two persons dancing together" and "one of two players on the same team." There is also a nautical reference to the word partner as "one of the reinforcing timbers used to support a mast."

All of these definitions have meaning that can be applied to a marriage relationship. We share both the profits, joys, and satisfactions; and we share the risks, losses, and failures of a two-person association. We engage in dance-like situations where we balance our movements to match our spouse's and discover we are lacking in rhythm. We get into games where we want to win and expect our teammate to play with us to achieve the goal. Partnership is loaded with implications we don't consider until they hit our little boat mid ship like a gale-force wind. Then we begin to understand the importance of together supporting the same cause like reinforcing timbers to a main mast.

*L*ike separate strings of a lute that quiver with the same music, there is beauty in a marriage that respects the individuality of its partners.

—Drs. Les & Leslie Parrott

*I*t's important to build a good relationship with your spouse so that when the children leave, you have the underlying joy of focusing on each other and not on your adult children.

—Wife married for thirty-five years

A companionship marriage is one in which both spouses are encouraged to maximize their strengths for the benefit of the couple.

—David & Claudia Arp

*W*ounds from a friend can be trusted.

—*Proverbs 27:6*

*W*armth is the friendly acceptance of a person, the feeling that a person is important enough for your time and effort. Empathy is the ability to understand.

—-Gary Smalley

*H*e who sows courtesy reaps friendship, and he who plants kindness gathers love.

—St. Basil

*U*nselfish love is an action directed toward fulfilling another person's needs.

—Gary Smalley

*H*e is happiest, king or peasant, who finds his peace at home.

—Goethe

*C*arry each other's burdens, and in this way you will fulfill the law of Christ.

—*Galatians 6:2*

*P*erfume and incense bring joy to the heart, and the pleasantness of one's friend springs from his earnest counsel.

—*Proverbs 27:9*

*M*arriage challenges us to new heights and calls us to be the best person possible, but neither marriage nor our partner will magically make us whole.

—*Drs. Les & Leslie Parrott*

*T*o make the world a friendly place, one must show it a friendly face.

—*James Whitcomb Riley*

*G*enuine love has no qualifications. It doesn't say, "I'll be your friend if you'll be mine" nor "I want to be your friend because your family is rich." This love does not seek to gain, but only to give.

—*Gary Smalley*

*M*ost negative people feel they could be positive if they had a different job, lived in a better place, or married a different person. But happiness does not hinge on better circumstances. A person with bad attitudes will still be a person with bad attitudes, wherever and with whomever he or she lives.

—Drs. Les & Leslie Parrott

*B*lessed are all who fear the LORD, who walk in his ways.

You will eat the fruit of your labor; blessings and prosperity will be yours.

Your wife will be like a fruitful vine within your house; your sons will be like olive shoots around your table.

Thus is the man blessed who fears the LORD.

May the LORD bless you from Zion all the days of your life; may you see the prosperity of Jerusalem, and may you live to see your children's children. Peace be upon Israel.

—*Psalm 128:1–6*

Prayer for Spiritual Partnership

*L*ord, help me to see my beloved as you do.

Help me to look with eyes of grace

and hear with humility.

Please give us your wisdom

to see our life together from the wide perspective

of heaven

instead of from our small lens

smeared by petty

grievances and complaints.

Help us to join in partnership with you and your

goals for our lives

so we can be part of your plan of love for this

world.

Help us to be a team that encourages our family

and those we meet and work with every day.

Help us be part of your solution for every life we

touch.

And help us to touch each other's life

with the same care you would use.

Amen

A friend loves at all times.

—*Proverbs 17:17*

I always pray with joy because of your partnership in the gospel from the first day until now, being confident of this, that he who began a good work in you will carry it on to completion until the day of Christ Jesus. It is right for me to feel this way about all of you, since I have you in my heart.

—*Philippians 1:3–7*

How good and pleasant it is when brothers live together in unity!
It is like precious oil poured on the head, running down on the beard, running down on Aaron's beard, down upon the collar of his robes.
It is as if the dew of Hermon were falling on Mount Zion. For there the LORD bestows his blessing, even life forevermore.

—*Psalm 133:1–3*

Wisdom

Becomes

You

Gaining Wisdom

*T*he soul of your marriage yearns for depth. At least three classic disciplines of the spiritual life call soul mates to move beyond surface living and into the depth: worship, service, and prayer. In the midst of our normal daily activities, these disciplines have a transforming power to quiet the spirit and nurture our marriage. By the way, these disciplines are not for spiritual giants, nor are they some dull drudgery designed to extinguish all the fun in your life. The only requirement to practice these disciplines is a longing for God to fill your marriage.

—Drs. Les & Leslie Parrott

*W*e usually find it easy, or at least necessary, to have a positive attitude around our friends and associates. Don't you agree that our mates deserve the same consideration?

—Gary Smalley

*H*e who covers over an offense promotes love, but whoever repeats the matter separates close friends.

—*Proverbs 17:9*

*L*ast, try to abandon "I told you so" statements. No matter how it's said, if it means "I told you so," eliminate it from your vocabulary. Such statements reflect an arrogance and self-centered-ness that can be harmful to your marriage.

—Gary Smalley

*N*o pessimist ever discovered the secrets of the stars, or sailed to an uncharted land, or opened a new heaven to the human spirit.

—Helen Keller

*L*et love and faithfulness never leave you. Write them on the tablet of your heart.

—*Proverbs 3:3*

*L*et us learn together what is good.

—*Job 34:4*

*T*each me your way, O LORD, and I will walk in your truth; give me an undivided heart.

—Psalm 86:11

*W*isdom—that elusive quest. We have so long searched for something big—lots of knowledge, a reputation as a wise person, a vast reservoir of wisdom. We have an amazing treasure right at hand to teach us the way to be wise. The Bible is our primary source of wisdom. In it are the instructions for knowing and following God. It holds the principles of right living that when fol-lowed will make us exceptional spouses. Open the Book, take small bites of the Word of God and consider the promises God makes to those who seek his wisdom like a lost pearl of great value.

*P*aul emphasized having oneness of spirit and mind in the church. He likened the struggle for oneness to an athlete striving to reach the goal (Phil. 1:27). Likewise, as husbands and wives we can learn to enter into a oneness or agreement.

—Gary Smalley

*U*nderstanding is a fountain of life to those who have it.

—Proverbs 16:22

*E*very vocation is holy to the Lord. Our vocation, or work, is an extension of our personal relationship with God. Ninety-five percent of us will never be in "occupational" ministry, but that doesn't mean we are not ministers.

—Patrick Morley

*W*herever we are, whatever our background is, whether we are old or young, single or married, Jesus wants us to know and serve him. We are his beloved, unique in all creation, with gifts and talents entrusted to our care for God's greater glory.

—Debra Evans

*O*ur people must learn to devote themselves to doing what is good, in order that they may provide for daily necessities and not live unproductive lives.

—Titus 3:14

*C*ommand them to do good, to be rich in good deeds, and to be generous and willing to share.

—1 Timothy 6:18

*F*or 60.7 percent of married women, helping their husbands means working outside the home. Financial help is certainly support. For others, it means managing their home while their husbands win the bread.

—Patrick Morley

*B*y wisdom the LORD laid the earth's foundations, by understanding he set the heavens in place; by his knowledge the deeps were divided, and the clouds let drop the dew. Preserve sound judgment and discernment, do not let them out of your sight; they will be life for you, an ornament to grace your neck. Then you will go on your way in safety, and your foot will not stumble; when you lie down, you will not be afraid; when you lie down, your sleep will be sweet. Have no fear of sudden disaster … for the LORD will be your confidence.

—Proverbs 3:19-26

$\mathcal{L}$ook around and find a couple who could be mentors for your marriage. Think about what you want your marriage to look like when you've been married for fifty or more years. How would you define "finishing well" for your marriage? Now is the time to invest in your marriage. Later you will reap the rewards. You may even become a mentor to younger couples.

—David & Claudia Arp

$\mathcal{Y}$ou are a letter from Christ, written not with ink but with the Spirit.

—*2 Corinthians 3:3*

$\mathcal{S}$o then, just as you received Christ Jesus as Lord, continue to live in him, rooted and built up in him, strengthened in the faith as you were taught, and overflowing with thankfulness.

—*Colossians 2:6-7*

$\mathcal{T}$he Lord will instruct you and teach you in the way you should go; [he] will counsel you and watch over you.

—*Psalm 32:8*

*C*ourage is the inner commitment to pursue a worthwhile goal without giving up hope. ... Persistence means continuing to pursue a goal until it is achieved.

—Gary Smalley

*T*his is a trustworthy saying. And I want you to stress these things, so that those who have trusted in God may be careful to devote themselves to doing what is good. These things are excellent and profitable for everyone.

—*Titus 3:8*

*T*herefore, as God's chosen people, holy and dearly loved, clothe yourselves with compassion, kindness, humility, gentleness, and patience. Bear with each other and forgive whatever grievances you may have against one another. Forgive as the Lord forgave you.

—*Colossians 3:12-13*

*W*hatever you do, work at it with all your heart, as working for the Lord, not for men.

—*Colossians 3:23*

*A*fter twenty years of marriage, I finally realized my husband will never be home at five P.M. While this is disappointing to me, I simply had to let that expectation go.

—Wife married for twenty-five years

*J*esus said both in words and by example that anyone who wishes to be leader or ruler must first learn to be servant of all (Matthew 20:26-27). Leaders are lovers. They serve—submit to—and listen to those whom they would lead.

When a husband is loving his wife with understanding, gentleness, warmth, and communication, it is relatively easy for her to submit to him as a person.

—Gary Smalley

*L*et love and faithfulness never leave you… write them on the tablet of your heart.

—*Proverbs 3:3*

*T*each me your way, O LORD, and I will walk in your truth; give me an undivided heart.

—*Psalm 86:11*

$\mathcal{G}$od has purpose: the entire Bible proclaims this. What matters is that his plan should be understood and fulfilled. ... The question is no longer whether one is succeeding or failing but whether one is fulfilling God's purpose or not, whether one is adventuring with him or against him.

—Paul Tournier

$\mathcal{F}$or he who is least among you all—he is the greatest.

—Luke 9:48

$\mathcal{M}$arriage is filled with both enjoyable and tedious tradeoffs, but by far the most dramatic loss experienced in a new marriage is the idealized image you have of your partner. ... But eventually, married life asked us to look reality square in the face and reckon with the fact that we did not marry the person we thought we did. ... Debunking the myth of eternal romance will do more than just about anything to help you build a lifelong, happy marriage.

—Drs. Les & Leslie Parrott

$\mathscr{R}$obert Frost observed that love (like a good poem) *begins in delight and ends in wisdom.*

He meant that ecstasy cannot stand still because it has a life of its own. It must move on hopefully, in the direction of wisdom.

—Ed Wheat, *The First Years of Forever*

$\mathscr{A}$ man's wisdom gives him patience.

—*Proverbs 19:11*

$\mathscr{I}$n accordance with the riches of God's grace that he lavished on us with all wisdom and under-standing. … he made known to us the mystery of his will according to his good pleasure, which he purposed in Christ, to be put into effect when the times will have reached their fulfillment—to bring all things in heaven and on earth together under one head, even Christ.

—*Ephesians 1:7-10*

$\mathscr{A}$ marital relationship that endures and becomes more fulfilling for both the husband and the wife is no accident.

—Gary Smalley

*Y*ou can trust [God] to be intimately involved in your efforts to develop a love-filled marriage.

It is possible for any Christian couple to develop this love relationship in their marriage because it is in harmony with God's express will.

Enjoy the *feelings* of love and guard them well, but live by the *facts* of love.

*Keep the delights of your love
ever-green and growing
by planting their roots deep into truth
and watering them with wisdom.*

—Ed Wheat

*T*he feelings of love cannot survive alone. They must be accompanied by the facts of love. Then "walking on air" becomes moving ahead together on solid ground, and delight is transformed by wisdom into something even better.

—Ed Wheat

*T*he LORD changes times and seasons…. He gives wisdom to the wise and knowledge to the discerning.

—*Daniel 2:21*

$\mathscr{T}$he recipe for success in marriage is effort plus insight.

—David & Vera Mace

$\mathscr{O}$ur friendship has grown into an intimacy that makes it seem like we've been together forever. It still amazes me when you know what I'm going to say, before I utter the words. Or when you realize my deepest needs and fears.

I want to protect what we share. And when I pray for you—for us—I place our love gently, safely in God's hands.

—Beth Swanson

$\mathscr{U}$nderstanding is a fountain of life to those who have it.

—*Proverbs 16:22*

$\mathscr{A}$ wise man's heart guides his mouth, and his lips promote instruction.

—*Proverbs 16:23*

Love does not brood over injuries. It keeps no record of wrongs because it cannot survive in doing so. Love knows that keeping track of tit for tat never brings equilibrium to an out-of-balance relationship. Love understands that wrongs are part of life and that no record can ever right them. Instead, the power of love is found in letting go of our record keeping. It loosens our grip on past pain and drives us to a fresh start. Love lets the history die and gives birth to a new beginning. It surrenders the compulsion to clear up every mis-understanding and lets the ledgers stay unbal-anced. Love prefers to let forgiveness heal former hurts so that we can focus on the future.

—Drs. Les and Leslie Parrott

I can do everything through Christ who gives me strength.

—*Philippians 4:13*

Apply your heart to instruction and your ears to words of knowledge. … There is surely a future hope for you, and your hope will not be cut off.

—*Proverbs 23:12, 18*

*T*he discerning heart seeks knowledge.

—Proverbs 15:14

*I*n everything, by prayer and petition, with thanksgiving, present your requests to God. And the peace of God, which transcends all understanding, will guard your hearts and your minds in Christ Jesus.

—Philippians 4:6–7

*T*he LORD is my helper; I will not be afraid.

—Hebrews 13:6

*T*he wise in heart are called discerning.

—Proverbs 16:21

A heart at peace gives life to the body.

—Proverbs 14:30

*R*emember your leaders, who spoke the word of God to you. Consider the outcome of their way of life and imitate their faith.

—Hebrews 13:7

*J*esus Christ is the same yesterday and today and forever.

—Hebrews 13:8

*A*s for God, his way is perfect; the word of the LORD is flawless. He is a shield for all who take refuge in him.

—2 Samuel 22:31

*C*ommit to the LORD whatever you do, and your plans will succeed.

—Proverbs 16:3

*S*how me your ways, O LORD, teach me your paths; guide me in your truth and teach me, for you are God my Savior, and my hope is in you all day long.

—Psalm 25:4

*T*he fear of the LORD is the beginning of wisdom; all who follow his precepts have good understanding.

—Psalm 111:10

*K*nowledge increases strength.

—*Proverbs 24:5*

*B*lessed is the man who does not walk in the counsel of the wicked or stand in the way of sinners or sit in the seat of mockers. But his delight is in the law of the LORD, and on his law he meditates day and night. He is like a tree planted by streams of water.

—*Psalm 1:1–3*

*G*race and peace be yours in abundance through the knowledge of God and of Jesus our Lord.

—*2 Peter 1:2*

*S*trength of character may be acquired at work, but beauty of character is learned at home. There the affections are trained. There the gentle life reaches us, the true heaven life. In one word, the family circle is the supreme conductor of Christianity.

—Henry Drummond

*P*eacemakers who sow in peace raise a harvest of righteousness.

—*James 3:18*

*W*ho is wise and understanding among you? Let him show it by his good life, by deeds done in the humility that comes from wisdom.

—*James 3:13*

*T*each me knowledge and good judgment, for I believe in your commands.

—*Psalm 119:66*

*F*or the multitude of world friends profiteth not, nor may strong helpers anything avail, nor wise counselors give profitable counsel, nor the cunning of doctors give consolation, nor riches deliver in time of need . . . if Thou, Lord, do not assist, help, comfort, counsel, inform, and defend.

—Thomas á Kempis

*W*here then does wisdom come from?
    Where does understanding dwell?

It is hidden from the eyes of every living thing,
    concealed even from the birds of the
air....

God understands the way to it
    and he alone knows where it dwells,
    for he views the ends of the earth
    and sees everything under the heavens.

When he established the force of the wind
    and measured out the waters,

when he made a decree for the rain
    and a path for the thunderstorm,

then he looked at wisdom and appraised it;
    he confirmed it and tested it.

And he said to man,
    'The fear of the Lord—that is wisdom,
and to shun evil is understanding.'

                                    —Job 28:20, 21, 23-28

*Y*ou make me glad by your deeds, O Lord; I sing for joy.

—Psalm 92:4

*T*he peace of God, which transcends all under-standing, will guard your hearts and your minds in Christ Jesus.

—Philippians 4:7

*G*od has said, "Never will I leave you; never will I forsake you."

—Hebrews 13:5

"*L*earn from me, for I am gentle and humble in heart, and you will find rest for your souls."

—Matthew 11:29

*T*rue happiness
Consists not in the multitude of friends,
But in the worth and choice.

—Ben Jonson

*I*t is the promise of knowledge to speak and it is the privilege of wisdom to listen.

—The Poet at the Breakfast Table

*T*he Love we share means so much . . . It means we are willing to risk the deepest parts of ourselves to know and love each other better.

It means we'll never end an argument without forgiveness or face an adversity we can't overcome together with God. It means the people who we are today will grow and change, and so will our love.

—From *Letters to My Love*

*F*or the LORD your God will bless you in all your harvest and in all the work of your hands, and your joy will be complete.

—*Deuteronomy 16:15*

Wisdom's Value

*H*ow can a young man keep his way pure? By living according to your word.

I seek you with all my heart; do not let me stray from your commands.

I have hidden your word in my heart that I might not sin against you.

Praise be to you, O LORD; teach me your decrees.

With my lips I recount all the laws that come from your mouth.

I rejoice in following your statutes as one rejoices in great riches.

I meditate on your precepts and consider your ways.

I delight in your decrees; I will not neglect your word.

Do good to your servant, and I will live; I will obey your word.

Open my eyes that I may see wonderful things in your law.

I am a stranger on earth; do not hide your commands from me. My soul is consumed with longing for your laws at all times.

—*Psalm 119:9–20*

*T*he Spirit of God first imparts love; he next inspires hope, and then gives liberty.

—Dwight L. Moody

I pray also that the eyes of your heart may be enlightened in order that you may know the hope to which he has called you, the riches of his glorious inheritance in the saints, and his incomparably great power for us who believe.

—*Ephesians 1:18-19*

*H*ave your heart right with Christ, and he will visit you often, and so turn weekdays into Sundays, meals into sacraments, homes into temples, and earth into heaven.

—Charles H. Spurgeon

*E*very good and perfect gift is from above, coming down from the Father of the heavenly lights, who does not change like shifting shadows.

—*James 1:17*

$\mathcal{Y}$ou guide me with your counsel. ... Whom have I in heaven but you? And earth has nothing I desire besides you. My flesh and my heart may fail, but God is the strength of my heart and my portion forever.

—*Psalm 73:24-26*

$\mathcal{I}$will put my law in their minds and write it on their hearts. I will be their God, and they will be my people.

—*Jeremiah 31:33*

$\mathcal{T}$he feelings of love will always require your attention. Think of it as an investment that yields high returns. Five or seven years down the road your love relationship will reveal just how much both of you have put into it.

—Ed Wheat, *The First Years of Forever*

$\mathcal{H}$old on to instruction, do not let it go; guard it well, for it is your life.

—*Proverbs 4:13*

*D*o not forget the things your eyes have seen or let them slip from your heart as long as you live. Teach them to your children and to their children after them.

—*Deuteronomy 4:9*

*H*ow much better to get wisdom than gold, to choose understanding rather than silver!

—*Proverbs 16:16*

A man who governs his passions is master of the world. We must either command them, or be enslaved by them. It is better to be a hammer than an anvil.

—St. Dominic

*W*e all suffer from feelings of self-doubt, unworthiness, and inadequacy.

—Drs. Les & Leslie Parrott

*I*s not this the kind of fasting I have chosen: to loose the chains of injustice and untie the cords of the yoke, to set the oppressed free and break every yoke? Is it not to share your food with the hungry and to provide the poor wanderer with shelter — when you see the naked, to clothe him, and not to turn away from your own flesh and blood? Then your light will break forth like the dawn, and your healing will quickly appear; then your righteousness will go before you, and the glory of the LORD will be your rear guard. Then you will call, and the LORD will answer; you will cry for help, and he will say: Here am I. If you do away with the yoke of oppression, with the pointing finger and malicious talk, and if you spend yourselves in behalf of the hungry and satisfy the needs of the oppressed, then your light will rise in the darkness, and your night will become like the noonday. The LORD will guide you always; he will satisfy your needs in a sun-scorched land and will strengthen your frame. You will be like a well-watered garden, like a spring whose waters never fail. Your people will rebuild the ancient ruins and will raise up the age-old foundations; you will be called Repairer of Broken Walls, Restorer of Streets with Dwellings.

—Isaiah 58:6–12

*N*ow faith is being sure of what we hope for and certain of what we do not see.

—Hebrews 11:1

*D*o not forsake wisdom, and she will protect you; love her, and she will watch over you.

—Proverbs 4:6

*W*isdom is more precious than rubies, and nothing you desire can compare with her.

—Proverbs 8:11

*I*n everything set them an example by doing what is good. … show integrity, seriousness and soundness of speech.

—Titus 2:7-8

*F*ollow the way of love.

—1 Corinthians14:1

*S*erve the Lord with wholehearted devotion and with a willing mind.

—1 Chronicles 28:9

Having Fun

It's Important!

So many words have been written about love and marriage. High-sounding and idealistic themes abound, but one of the best things about marriage is the simple fun of being with someone you love. Just hanging out. Sticking around to see what will happen next. Watching clouds pass over. Listening for the next words from our beloved's mouth.

Observing the lift of the eyebrow when surprised, or the curl of the tongue licking at a favorite ice cream flavor. Just the joy and fun of everything that makes up this beloved person. Nothing more is needed to have fun.

When we bring sunshine into the lives of others, we're warmed by it ourselves. When we spill a little happiness, it splashes on us.

—Barbara Johnson

Like two fine pages
*   become one*
We refuse to open
*   to be read or writ upon*
What lovely, listing lines

*   would fate endow*

If we should dare
*   to read aloud?*

—Pat Matuszak

In biblical times, the special status of "bride and groom" lasted a full year. "If a man has recently married, he must not be sent to war or have any other duty laid on him. For one year he is to be free to stay at home and bring happiness to the wife he has married." The beginning of marriage was a time of learning and adapting. It still is. So allow yourself the same luxury.

—Drs. Les & Leslie Parrott

A cheerful heart is good medicine.

—*Proverbs 17:22*

$\mathscr{I}$t is not how much we have, but how much we enjoy, that makes happiness.

—Charles H. Spurgeon

$\mathscr{S}$piritual healing isn't always found in a formal worship service. Fun can heal and our knowledge that God is the source of joy opens our eyes to his presence in the daily humorous events that surprise us and cause us to laugh when we were just on the verge of tears or sighs.

Over the last two decades, marriage specialists have researched the ingredients of a happy marriage. As a result, we know more about building a successful marriage today than ever before. For example, happily married couples will have:

Healthy expectations of marriage
A realistic concept of love
A positive attitude and outlook toward life
The ability to communicate their feelings
And understanding and acceptance of their gender differences
The ability to make decisions and settle arguments
A common spiritual foundation and goal

—Drs. Les & Leslie Parrott

*H*aving a healthy, growing marriage relationship requires friendship, fun, and romance. … Great dates are more than going to a movie and tuning out the world for a while. Great dates involve communicating with one another, reviving the spark that initially ignited your fire, and developing mutual interests and goals that are not focused on your careers or your children. Great dates can revitalize your relationship.

—David & Claudia Arp

*S*ay to God, "How awesome are your deeds! So great is your power that your enemies cringe before you. All the earth bows down to you; they sing praise to you, they sing praise to your name." Selah.

Come and see what God has done, how awesome his works in man's behalf! He turned the sea into dry land, they passed through the waters on foot — come, let us rejoice in him. …Praise our God, O peoples, let the sound of his praise be heard.

—*Psalm 66:3–8*

*H*ome interprets heaven; Home is heaven for beginners.

—Charles Henry Parkhurst

*Y*ou cannot always have happiness, but you can always give happiness.

—Anonymous

*S*ometimes a light surprises
The Christian while he sings;
It is the Lord who rises
With healing on His wings.

—William Cowper

*C*ome to me, all you who are weary and burdened, and I will give you rest.

—*Matthew 11:28*

*W*e are trying to put more fun in our lives. And to do the unexpected is a great boredom preventer.

—Sarah McCracken

*M*y heart leaps for joy and I will give thanks to [the LORD] in song.

—*Psalm 28:7*

*E*ven the best marriages take a tremendous amount of work. If there is no fun to balance out the work, even the most earnest spouses begin to lose motivation and energy. And the more challenging a marriage is, the more important fun is. We have learned that mutually enjoyable, fun experiences can help heal tender wounds and become a bridge across frustrating differences.

—Bill & Lynne Hybels

*Y*ou will go out in joy and be led forth in peace; the mountains and hills will burst into song before you, and all the trees of the field will clap their hands.

—*Isaiah 55:12*

*G*ive what you have. To someone else it may be better than you dare to think.

—Henry Wadsworth Longfellow

Under the greenwood tree
    Who loves to lie with me?
    And turn his merry note
    Unto the sweet bird's throat,

Come hither, come hither, come hither;
    Here shall he see
    No enemy

But winter and rough weather.
    Who doth ambition shun
    And loves to lie i' the sun,
    Seeking the food he eats
    And pleased with what he gets,

Come hither, come hither, come hither;
    Here shall he see
    No enemy

But winter and rough weather.

—William Shakespeare

*W*hen I found the one my heart loves,
I held him and would not let him go . . .
Daughters of Jerusalem, I charge you
by the gazelles and by the does of the field:
Do not arouse or awaken love
until it so desires.

—*Song of Songs 3:4–5*

*T*he unthankful heart . . . discovers no mercies;
but the thankful heart . . . will find, in every hour,
some heavenly blessings.

—Henry Ward Beecher

*M*y child—Star—you gaze at the stars,
And I wish I were the firmament
That I might watch you with many eyes.

—Plato

A *Sense* OF *Humor* *Saves* THE *Day*

*O*ur laughter binds us together as husband and wife.

—Gary Smalley

*A*n attorney we know who handles many divorce cases told us that the Number One reason two people split up is that they "refuse to accept the fact that they are married to a *human being.*"

—Drs. Les & Leslie Parrott

I've decided to get into a good humor and stay that way. That's why I've decided to treat people with kindness and a smile whenever I meet them, regardless of how they treat me. ... One way I let my joy out is to give people something to laugh about. I collect jokes and write down everything I hear that makes me brighten up. I make amusement a ministry.

—Barbara Johnson

$\mathcal{T}$hank God for dirty dishes; they have a tale to tell
While other folks go hungry, we're eating pretty well.
With home, and health, and happiness, we shouldn't want to fuss
For by this stack of evidence, God's very good to us.

—Anonymous

$\mathcal{I}$f laughter doesn't come naturally for you, here are some pointers that may help you become more jovial.

Give Yourself Permission to Be Less Than Perfect.

When you don't take yourself so seriously, you can relax, and it is easier to laugh and see the lighter side of life.

Cultivate Humor. We place cartoons and jokes on our refrigerator door and try to look for the humor in each situation....

Get Some Funny Friends. If you're both the sober type, find some funny couples to get to know.

—David & Claudia Arp

$\mathcal{I}$ will refresh the weary and satisfy the faint.

—Jeremiah 31:25

A pleasant word is a bright ray of sunshine on a saddened heart.

Therefore, give others the sunshine, and tell Jesus the rest.

—L.B. Cowman

*O*ur feelings follow our thinking and/or actions. If our thinking and actions are positive, then our feelings will be positive in a matter of hours (The scriptures teach that as a person "thinks within himself, so is he"[Proverbs 23:7]).

—Gary Smalley

*H*appiness does not depend on outward things, but on the way we see them.

—Leo Tolstoy

*O*ur mouths were filled with laughter, our tongues with songs of joy. Then it was said among the nations, "The LORD has done great things for them." The LORD has done great things for us, and we are filled with joy.

—*Psalm 126:2-3*

*W*hen one door of happiness closes, another opens; but often we look so long at the closed door that we do not see the one which has been opened for us.

—Helen Keller

*T*he joy of the LORD is your strength.

—*Nehemiah 8:10*

*M*y mistress' eyes are nothing like the sun,
Coral is far more red, than her lips red,
If snow be white, why then her breasts are dun;
If hairs be wires, black wires grow on her head;
I have seen roses damasked, red and white,
But no such roses see I in her cheeks,
And in some perfumes is there more delight,
Than in the breath that from my mistress reeks,
I love to hear her speak, yet well I know,
that music hath a far more pleasing sound;
I grant I never saw a goddess go,
My mistress when she walks treads on the ground.
And yet by heaven I think my love as rare,
As any she belied with false compare.

—William Shakespeare

*C*huckles are better than a therapist. They are aloe vera for the sunburns of life. ... When the dumps take their toll, laughter provides the exact change to get you through.

—Barbara Johnson

*T*here is nothing holier,
in this life of ours,
than the first consciousness of love—
the first fluttering of its silken wings.

—Henry Wadsworth Longfellow

*T*he love we share means so much ... It means we are willing to risk the deepest parts of ourselves to know and love each other better.

It means we'll never end an argument without forgiveness or face an adversity we can't overcome together with God. It means the people who we are today will grow and change, and so will our love.

—Beth Swanson

I run in the path of your commands, for you have set my heart free.

—*Psalm 119:32*

A gentle answer turns away wrath, but a harsh word stirs up anger.

—*Proverbs 15:1*

A happy heart makes the face cheerful, but heartache crushes the spirit.

—*Proverbs 15:13*

*A*ll the days of the oppressed are wretched, but the cheerful heart has a continual feast.

—*Proverbs 15:15*

*B*etter a little with the fear of the LORD than great wealth with turmoil.

—*Proverbs 15:17*

A man finds joy in giving an apt reply—and how good is a timely word!

—*Proverbs 15:23*

Getting TO Know You

In marriage we still sometimes dance around each other much as we first did during the early days of our courtship—hesitantly, carefully. Does our partner really want to participate? Do I really know the steps? But the more we get to know one another, the more we can grow in trust of each other. Then we can move along together through life in a rhythm that is unique to our marriage. Then deep places in our spirit call to those in our beloved just like the Holy Spirit calls to us both —together and separately.

Many couples, thinking they know each other intimately, have actually lived on a superficial level for years. Unfortunately, marriages of this type are the norm rather than the exception.

—Gary Smalley

*T*he emotional side of love's triangle is intimacy. Love without intimacy is only a hormonal illusion. One cannot desire another person over the long haul without really *knowing* that person.

—Drs. Les & Leslie Parrott

*C*elebrate your differences.

—Patrick Morley

*H*e says *"To him who overcomes, I will give ... a white stone with a new name written on it, known only to him who receives it."*

—Revelation 2:17

*J*esus calls to you in the night, as you lie down to sleep. He calls to you in the morning when you awake. Let yourself hear him. Listen for the voice of the good shepherd, calling you by name.

—Edith Bajema

The Night-Wind

I said, "Go, gentle singer,
Thy wooing voice is kind,
But do not think its music
Has power to reach my mind.

"Play with the scented flower,
The young tree's supple bough,
And leave my human feelings
In their own course to flow."

The wanderer would not leave me;
Its kiss grew warmer still—
"O come," it sighed so sweetly,
"I'll win thee 'gainst thy will.

"Have we not been from childhood friends?
Have I not loved thee long?
As long as thou hast loved the night
Whose silence wakes my song."

—Emily Brontë

*D*eep calls to deep in the roar of your waterfalls; all your waves and breakers have swept over me. By day the LORD directs his love, at night his song is with me — a prayer to the God of my life.

—Psalm 42:7–8

*W*hen love is real love,
When people's souls go out to their beloved,
When they lose their hearts to them,
When they act in the unselfish way
In which these exquisite
Old English phrases denote,
A miracle is produced.

—Ernest Dimnet

*A*nyone without a soul friend is like a body without a head.

—Celtic saying

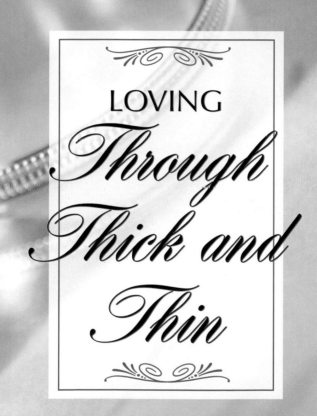

LOVING

Through

Thick and

Thin

In Good Times and...

*N*early all of us enter marriage believing our love for our mate will never fade. Yet in the U.S. today, for every two marriages, there is one divorce. For too long we have accepted Hollywood's portrayal of love as the type of love for which to strive. It doesn't take long to discover that mere passion which revolves around sexual gratification is not sufficient in itself to establish a lasting relationship. Unfortunately, too many couples begin their marriages thinking this type of love is all they need.

There are at least three types of love—affection, passion, and genuine love—only the latter provides an adequate foundation for the other two types.

—Gary Smalley

$\mathcal{T}$he honeymoon stage is a time of anticipation, establishing routines, setting up house, getting to know each other in a new way, silly and selfish conflicts, pursuing dreams, establishing employment, and just generally having fun together.

—Patrick Morley

$\mathcal{L}$ove does not delight in evil but rejoices with the truth. It always protects, always trusts, always hopes, always perseveres. Love never fails.

—*1 Corinthians 13:6-8*

$\mathcal{P}$leasant memories and treasured traditions can provide building blocks upon which a young couple can build their own marriage and family life.

—Bill & Lynne Hybels

$\mathcal{I}$f you expect your love affair to remain the same or count on it to get better and better without effort on your part, you will be disappointed. Your love relationship must change because it is a living entity.

—Ed Wheat

$\mathscr{J}$ust as an actor in a dramatic performance follows a script, so do married couples. Without knowing it, a bride and groom are drawn into acting out roles that they form from a blend of their personal dispositions, family backgrounds, and marital expectations. … Once you are aware of the roles you each tend to take, you can then discuss how to write a new script together

—Drs. Les & Leslie Parrott

$\mathscr{F}$or I have learned to be content whatever the circumstances. I know what it is to be in need, and I know what it is to have plenty. I have learned the secret of being content in any and every situation. … I can do everything through him who gives me strength.

—Philippians 4:11-13

$\mathscr{C}$onsider how the lilies grow. They do not labor or spin. Yet I tell you, not even Solomon in all his splendor was dressed like one of these. If that is how God clothes the grass of the field … how much more will he clothe you?"

—Luke 12:27-28

*J*esus answered, "Do not let your hearts be troubled. Trust in God; trust also in me."

—*John 14:1*

*T*here are thorns and thistles in life, and God put them there for our benefit and because he loves us. Thorns and thistles are the way we grow.

—Patrick Morley

*T*he best way to describe the building stage is to say that energy is directed toward vocation rather than communication. While this phase is tough on marriage, communication can be improved vastly by carving out time to be alone together, learning to be frank about your needs and desires for time and conversation, being interested in what your mate is interested in, and planning in advance some questions to ask your spouse.

—Patrick Morley

*T*he problem with life is that it is so daily.

—Patrick Morley

$\mathscr{O}$ne of our problems is that marriage today is taken so lightly. … The couple who has under-girded their marriage by their commitment will be prepared for those inevitable times when their marriage will be tested.

—Ed Wheat

$\mathscr{P}$robably the most widely believed of all the marriage myths is this one: Marriage will ensure my happiness.

—Bill & Lynne Hybels

$\mathscr{T}$he LORD is my shepherd, I shall not be in want. He makes me lie down in green pastures, he leads me beside quiet waters, he restores my soul. He guides me in paths of righteousness for his name's sake.

—Psalm 23:1-3

$\mathscr{J}$esus said, "I have told you these things, so that in me you may have peace. In this world you will have trouble. But take heart! I have overcome the world."

—John 16:33

*M*arriages can never be perfect because people are not perfect. So, how can a couple live happily ever after? Not by depending on externals. ... You need a sense of mastery, of control; the feeling that something good has happened because you *caused* it to happen.

Living happily ever after only works when you *make* it work.

—Drs. Les & Leslie Parrott

*M*ay your unfailing love come to me, O LORD.

—Psalm 119:41

*S*trengthen the feeble hands, steady the knees that give way; say to those with fearful hearts, "Be strong, do not fear; your God will come."

—Isaiah 35:3-4

*Y*ou have to accept whatever comes and the only important thing is that you meet it with courage and the best you have to give.

—Eleanor Roosevelt

*G*enuine love does not depend upon emotions or circumstances. It takes full advantage of the present to bring meaning and joy to the lives of others. If your marriage is to become all that you long for, you must begin today, right now, to develop the unconditional love which forms the foundation of a fulfilling marriage.

—Gary Smalley

*T*he forever relationship does not have to be a dream that vanishes in the light of cold, hard day. In fact, it will actually thrive on adversity and become more precious when the rest of life has temporarily lost its joy. ... It cannot be found or fallen into, but *formed*—by a man and a woman who want it enough to pour their lives into the building process.

—Ed Wheat

*T*hose who trust in the LORD are like Mount Zion, which cannot be shaken but endures forever.

—*Psalm 125:1*

*P*lace me like a seal over your heart, like a seal on your arm; for love is as strong as death, its jealousy unyielding as the grave. It burns like blazing fire, like a mighty flame. Many waters cannot quench love; rivers cannot wash it away. If one were to give all the wealth of his house for love, it would be utterly scorned.

—*Song of Songs 8:6-7*

*W*e also rejoice in our sufferings, because we know that suffering produces perseverance; perseverance, character; and character, hope. And hope does not disappoint us, because God has poured out his love into our hearts by the Holy Spirit, whom he has given us.

—*Romans 5:3-5*

*B*lessed is he whose help is the God of Jacob, whose hope is in the LORD his God.

—*Psalm 146:5*

$\mathcal{O}$ LORD, you have searched me and you know me. You know when I sit and when I rise. … You hem me in—behind and before; you have laid your hand upon me. … Where can I go from your Spirit? Where can I flee from your presence? If I go up to the heavens, you are there; if I make my bed in the depths, you are there. If I rise on the wings of the dawn, if I settle on the far side of the sea, even there your hand will guide me, your right hand will hold me fast. … For you created my inmost being; you knit me together in my mother's womb…. My frame was not hidden from you when I was made in the secret place. When I was woven together in the depths of the earth, your eyes saw my unformed body. All the days ordained for me were written in your book before one of them came to be.

—*Psalm 139: 1-2, 5, 7-10, 13, 15-16*

$\mathcal{R}$ esearch reveals that the level of a couple's joy is determined by each partner's ability to *adjust to things beyond his or her control.* Every happy couple has learned to find the right attitude in spite of the conditions they find themselves in.

—*Drs. Les & Leslie Parrott*

$\mathscr{A}$ perfectly charming college girl was talking to a much older married friend about the challenges of dating that she had faced in the past year at school. Her friend had an awful time holding in a hoot of laughter when the girl looked at her with envy and said, "You're so lucky to be married! Now all your troubles are over!" The older woman just smiled and remembered to pray for her young friend more often!

—Anonymous

$\mathscr{Y}$ our righteousness reaches to the skies, O God, you who have done great things. Who, O God, is like you? Though you have made me see troubles, many and bitter, you will restore my life again; from the depths of the earth you will again bring me up. You will increase my honor and comfort me once again. I will praise you with the harp for your faithfulness, O my God; I will sing praise to you with the lyre, O Holy One of Israel. My lips will shout for joy when I sing praise to you — I, whom you have redeemed. My tongue will tell of your righteous acts all day long, for those who wanted to harm me have been put to shame and confusion.

—*Psalm 71:19–24*

*T*he beautiful vision we see before our eyes as the wedding party gathers at the front of the church makes a nice photo for our wedding album. But we soon find out that "couplehood" is more like what happens when getting ready for the wedding than the photos we cherish after the wedding.

Think about it. Before the wedding, we trek all over town looking for flowers only to be frustrated when we find that the ones we want are way out of our price range. We find just the right clothing for our wedding party, only to be told the outfits we want are not available in the sizes and colors we need. It's one thing after another as we get ready for the big day and it seems to become more and more complicated as we proceed down our "to do" list. Married life can get to be like that, too. We start to purchase a house and find that the one we want is too high priced. We want to take a vacation and find we both have different destinations in mind. We plan to settle down and a job change takes us to a whole new place. Ideas, plans, dreams have to be adapted to conform to reality and we have to work together as a couple to adjust our dreams.

So whether we are getting ready for the wedding or learning the fine art of "couplehood" we must learn to keep a sense of humor and cultivate a willingness to exchange the ideal scenario for the possible one. We learn to look into each other's eyes and say, "That's okay. The important thing is we will be together in this."

I began to think about the biblical virtues of kindness and gentleness after my father-in-law handed me a note he received from my wife when she was a girl. In Esther's nine-year-old handwriting were these words: "Dear Dad, Please be nice to me." If my wife had to beg one of the nicest men I know to be nice to her, maybe being nice really does matter.

The apostle Paul urged us to be kind and gentle toward one another (Gal. 5:22–23). Sadly, I don't see either of these qualities in marriages much today. I don't see enough in my own marriage.

In Galatians, Paul uses fruit as a metaphor to describe what happens when Christ's spirit resides in our hearts. It is a funny thing, this Spirit. Give it freedom to dwell within you, and there's little room for the grouchy words and thoughtless acts that bedevil many marriages.

—Lyn Cryderman

Love

*L*ove bade welcome; yet my soul drew back,
    Guilty of dust and sin.
But quick-eyed Love, observing me grow slack
    From my first entrance in,

Drew nearer to me, sweetly questioning
    If I lacked anything.

"A guest," I answered, "worthy to be here":
    Love said, "You shall be he."
"I, the unkind, ungrateful? Ah, my dear,
    I cannot look on thee."
Love took my hand, and smiling did reply,
    "Who made the eyes but I?"

"Truth, LORD; but I have marred them; let my shame
    Go where it doth deserve."
"And know you not," says Love, "who bore the blame?"
    "My dear, then I will serve."

"You must sit down," says Love, "and taste my meat."
    So I did sit and eat.

—George Herbert

*L*ight beckons at the end of this passage—
    through cloud
    through sea
    through fire

Dim, foggy, steam-choked light—
Floating like a promise,
    this tiny, feathered beam
    that sings without ceasing.

We clutch hands to struggle
    through sand
    through wind
    through waves

Our crossing opens a path —
Shimmering through the midst of the sea.

—Pat Matuszak

*M*y soul finds rest in God alone.

—Psalm 62:1

*A*ll love is sweet, given or returned.
Common as light is love,
And its familiar voice wearies not ever . . .

—Percy Bysshe Shelley

$\mathcal{I}$ will sing of the LORD's great love forever; with my mouth I will make your faithfulness known through all generations.

I will declare that your love stands firm forever, that you established your faithfulness in heaven itself.

You said, "I have made a covenant with my chosen one, I have sworn to David my servant, 'I will establish your line forever and make your throne firm through all generations.' " Selah.

The heavens praise your wonders, O LORD, your faithfulness too, in the assembly of the holy ones.

For who in the skies above can compare with the LORD? Who is like the LORD among the heavenly beings?

In the council of the holy ones God is greatly feared; he is more awesome than all who surround him.

O LORD God Almighty, who is like you? You are mighty, O LORD, and your faithfulness surrounds you.

You rule over the surging sea; when its waves

mount up, you still them.

You crushed Rahab like one of the slain; with your strong arm you scattered your enemies.

The heavens are yours, and yours also the earth; you founded the world and all that is in it.

You created the north and the south; Tabor and Hermon sing for joy at your name.

Your arm is endued with power; your hand is strong, your right hand exalted.

Righteousness and justice are the foundation of your throne; love and faithfulness go before you.

Blessed are those who have learned to acclaim you, who walk in the light of your presence, O LORD.

They rejoice in your name all day long; they exult in your righteousness.

For you are their glory and strength, and by your favor you exalt our horn.

Indeed, our shield belongs to the LORD, our king to the Holy One of Israel.

—Psalm 89:1–18

$\mathscr{A}$ man once told me: "Every day my wife asks me if I really love her. I tell her I love her, but for some reason she doesn't believe I mean it. How can I help her feel secure about my love?"

This man's wife isn't all that unusual. One of the deepest universal human needs is the need for assurance that we're loved. The situation he described is one I've heard again and again. There's a lot of truth in the old saw "opposites attract." Often the differences emerge in the area of how we communicate our love. One partner is a romantic, and the other tends to be painfully practical. The practical one, usually the guy, is the sort of person whose idea of the perfect Christmas gift for his wife would be a set of snow tires for her car. After all, what could be more loving than providing for her safety? But his wife would prefer a romantic weekend get-away or a new silk blouse.

The romantic-practical balance can often enhance a marriage, so the solution is not for either partner to try to change the other. The most effective way to deal with situations like this is to see it, not as a personality problem, but as a simple "language barrier." The practical partner communicates love logically, often with performance as the basis of his expression of love. "Of course I love her: I pay the taxes, I work hard every day, I've never been unfaithful." To the practical partner, those things clearly say how much he loves his wife.

But for the romantic spouse, love is a language tied to the emotions. Loving actions evoke feelings in the heart, not just the head.

How does a marriage of opposites solve this problem? The same way a couple would if one of them spoke only German and the other spoke only English. You try to learn each other's language. Understanding a foreign language is easier than speaking it, but you need to work at both.

—Jay Kesler

So I say, live by the Spirit, and you will not gratify the desires of the sinful nature.

For the sinful nature desires what is contrary to the Spirit, and the Spirit what is contrary to the sinful nature. They are in conflict with each other, so that you do not do what you want.

But if you are led by the Spirit, you are not under law.

The acts of the sinful nature are obvious: sexual immorality, impurity and debauchery; idolatry and witchcraft; hatred, discord, jealousy, fits of rage, selfish ambition, dissensions, factions and envy; drunkenness, orgies, and the like. I warn you, as I did before, that those who live like this will not inherit the kingdom of God.
But the fruit of the Spirit is love, joy, peace, patience, kindness, goodness, faithfulness, gentleness and self-control. Against such things there is no law.
Those who belong to Christ Jesus have cruci-

fied the sinful nature with its passions and
desires. Since we live by the Spirit, let us
keep in step with the Spirit.
Let us not become conceited, provoking and
envying each other.

—*Galatians 5:16–26*

$\mathcal{W}$hen we have been in love
for many years,
I hope we'll spend Saturday mornings
sitting in the sunshine . . .
Holding hands when
we go for a walk . . .
Lying barefoot in the grass
when night falls
Listening to the crickets sing
and watching the stars twinkle
in the deep blue sky . . .
Knowing we have a love
that will last forever.

—Beth Swanson

Isn't It Romantic?

It's great when we plan a romantic outing and everything works together perfectly. What a triumph! At those time we feel as if we are the most suave, romantic couple on earth. We planned and pulled off a wonderful time for just the two of us. Then there's music in the air and all is right in God's world.

But what about the other times. So many elements seem to conspire to throw us off the track of romance. No matter how carefully we plan that dream date and guard it on our calendar, a car breaks down, guests drop in, someone gets sick, or it rains on our picnic day at the beach. Those times when the plan goes wrong, there is no sight more worth remembering than the smile of grace appearing in the eyes of our beloved—a smile that says, "It's OK. I feel as much love as if it had all gone perfectly." Those tender moments of love and understanding will stay with us much longer than the memories of a perfect romantic date.

*T*he courtship stage is a time of mutual fascination, curiosity, and attraction—in all ways. Couples enjoy long walks and longer talks, expressions of sensitivity come naturally, the warm glow of love abounds, and they cling to each other in syrupy displays of affection.

— Patrick Morley

*M*y lover spoke and said to me, "Arise, my darling, my beautiful one, and come with me. See! The winter is past; the rains are over and gone. Flowers appear on the earth; the season of singing has come."

—*Song of Songs 2:10-12*

*L*et him kiss me with the kisses of his mouth— for your love is more delightful than wine.

—*Song of Songs 1:2*

In our sexual relationship it's easy to become "me-centered" and lose our sensitivity to our partner. We forget that the best way to really please ourselves is to please our mate. When we focused on pleasing the other, we were less self-conscious. … Perhaps you will want to talk with each other about your love life. Do what you need to do to build a creative love life. It will enrich your marriage!

—David & Claudia Arp

Can the smoldering embers of dying feelings be refueled? We think they can be. We think that the love that drew a couple together in courtship can be recaptured and sustained, in spite of disappointments and setbacks and stormy weather. … Romance begins with knowledge of one another, and the key to knowledge is open, honest, consistent communication.

—Bill & Lynne Hybels

I love thee to the depth and breadth and height my soul can reach, when feeling out of sight.

—Elizabeth Barrett Browning

*Y*ou have stolen my heart, my sister, my bride; you have stolen my heart with one glance of your eyes, with one jewel of your necklace. How delightful is your love, my sister, my bride! How much more pleasing is your love than wine, and the fragrance of your perfume than any spice!

—*Song of Songs 4:9-10*

*T*ouch is one of God's most powerful forces. … Touch converts potential love into actual love. Touch releases power. It's like taking jumper cables and attaching a live battery to a dead battery. When we touch there is a transfer of energy from one person to the other. Sexual pleasure is a beautiful gift of God for married couples. Biblically speaking, sex is good! Sexual intimacy should bring the greatest bliss, joy, pleasure, oneness, and happiness of human life.

—Patrick Morley

*T*urn your eyes from me; they overwhelm me. Who is this that appears like the dawn, fair as the moon, bright as the sun, majestic as the stars in procession?

—*Song of Songs 6:5, 10*

*H*usbands and wives need to pinpoint their own and their spouse's preferred languages of love, and then negotiate a way to make sure they both receive love in the language they can understand. That often requires flexibility, sensitivity, and a willingness to grow in areas where we may be weak.

—Bill & Lynne Hybels

*H*ow do I love thee? Let me count the ways.
I love thee to the depth and breadth and height
My soul can reach, when feeling out of sight
For the ends of Being and ideal Grace.
I love thee to the level of every day's
Most quiet need, by sun and candle light.
I love thee freely, as men strive for right;
I love thee purely, as they turn from praise.
I love thee with the passion put to use
In my old griefs, and with my childhood's faith.
I love thee with a love I seemed to lose
With my lost saints!—I love thee with the breath,
Smiles, tears of all my life—and, if God choose,
I shall but love thee better after death.

—Elizabeth Barrett Browning

$\mathcal{D}$o the unexpected! …You can add the element of surprise by doing the unexpected. We've been known to do some zany things ourselves. Claudia will never forget the day Dave came in with three red roses and said, "Pack your bag. We're leaving in thirty minutes!"… Off we went to a wonderful little hotel in the mountains about an hour from where we lived. … If you're going to have a romantic affair, have it with your spouse!

—David & Claudia Arp

$\mathcal{D}$uring the first few years of marriage, most couples hit a wall. The particulars vary from one couple to the next, but the result is the same. A bewildered husband and wife look at each other and silently worry: "I thought I knew this person. How could I have missed all of these flaws? Is our marriage headed down the tubes?"

When the carefree idealism of early marriage gives way to the hard realities of life, your relationship may founder for a time. But if you remain true to your vows to love, honor and cherish each other for a lifetime, eventually you'll learn to accept—and even respect—your differences.

—Jim and Aldine Musser

Different Planets?

*C*an this person really live on the same earth and breathe the same air and not understand what we mean at all? It seems impossible sometimes, but men and women made by the same Creator, who go back to the same dust after taking long and twisting routes through life, can harbor very different views of ... well ... just about everything! Being one in marriage seems to signify more of a completing of two opposite halves rather than both coming to one side or the other of an issue. And this is just what calls us back to negotiate understanding, this incessant need to complete the puzzle together, even when we want to give up and lock all the doors and windows against its desire.

*M*aking assumptions about the language of love our spouse prefers often leads to disappointment, and sometimes even to misunderstanding.

—Bill & Lynne Hybels

The man said, "This is now bone of my bones and flesh of my flesh; she shall be called 'woman,' for she was taken out of man." For this reason a man will leave his father and mother and be united to his wife, and they will become one flesh.

—*Genesis 2:23-24*

The difference? She wants a soul mate; he wants a lover. Any couple can have a much improved sex life by understanding the sexual differences between husbands and wives.

—Patrick Morley

What exactly is this "woman's intuition?" It's not something mystical; rather, it is an unconscious perception of minute details that are sometimes tangible, sometimes abstract in nature. Since it is usually an "unconscious" process, many times a woman isn't able to give specific explanations for the way she feels. She simply perceives or "feels" something about a situation or person, while a man tends to follow logical analysis of circumstances or people.

—Gary Smalley

The natural course, if untended, is to drift apart and become the proverbial two ships passing in the night.

—Patrick Morley

Do we always agree …? Of course not, but we have learned to communicate, compromise, and develop our own plan. … Working together has been a plus.…Can you think of ways your differences give balance to your marriage partnership?

—David & Claudia Arp

Speaking the truth in love, we will in all things grow up into him who is the Head, that is, Christ. From him the whole body, joined and held together by every supporting ligament, grows and builds itself up in love, as each part does its work.

—*Ephesians 4:15-16*

The ideal marriage evolves when the wife concentrates on meeting her husband's needs and the husband concentrates on meeting his wife's needs. That combination builds the lasting qualities of a giving relationship.

—Gary Smalley

*F*riends cherish each other's hopes. They are kind to each other's dreams.

—Henry David Thoreau

*V*irtually all men believe that they are, or have been, a difficult husband to live with. …
Most men have it in their hearts to do the right thing. Based on hundreds of surveys and thousands of interviews I would say the overwhelming conclusion is this: Most men really want to do the right thing. Men deeply love their wives.

—Patrick Morley

*H*e who finds a wife finds what is good and receives favor from the LORD.

—*Proverbs 18:22*

*G*od put the man in a garden and said, "work and take care of this place." God noticed two problems. First, everything he had made was not only *good* but *very good,* except that the man was alone, and, well … that was *not* good. The first problem God recognized was that it was not good for man to be alone.

—Patrick Morley

Ten Commandments For Husbands

I.   *Treat Your Wife with Strength and Gentleness.*

II. *Give Ample Praise and Reassurance.*

III. *Define the Areas of Responsibility.*

IV. *Avoid Criticism.*

V.   *Remember the Importance of "Little Things."*

VI. *Recognize Her Need for Togetherness.*

VII. *Give Her a Sense of Security.*

VIII. *Recognize the Validity of Her Moods.*

IX. *Cooperate with Her in Every Effort to Improve Your Marriage.*

X.   *Discover Her Particular, Individual Needs and Try to Meet Them.*

Ten Commandments For Wives

I.   *Learn the Real Meaning of Love.*

II.   *Give Up Your Dreams of a "Perfect Marriage" and Work Toward a "Good Marriage."*

III.   *Discover Your Husband's Personal, Unique Needs and Try to Meet Them.*

IV.   *Abandon All Dependency Upon Your Parents and All Criticism of His Relatives.*

V.   *Give Praise and Appreciation Instead of Seeking It.*

VI.   *Surrender Possessiveness and Jealousy.*

VII.   *Greet Your Husband with Affection Instead of Complaints or Demands.*

VIII.   *Abandon All Hope of Changing Your Husband Through Criticism or Attack.*

IX.   *Outgrow the Princess Syndrome.*

X.   *Pray for Patience.*

—Cecil Osborne

The Best IS Yet TO Be...

*N*ot many young men going out to win a girl would decide to use the following strange proposal Robert Browning chooses in his famous poem. Imagine the fellow looking into the eyes of a girl in the prime of her beauty and the first winning thought that comes to his mind is "Let's get old together!" Getting old is the last thing on either of their minds! If anything, the couple probably feels as if they had both just been born. Now that they've found each other the world is all fresh and new.

Yet, Browning's poem has been cherished by couples over the years as a "romantic" tribute. Longtime lovers understand his thought as he draws the total and describes what becoming a couple adds up to in the end. Learning together, in many ways not just growing old but growing up. Being together—being there for each other.

𝒢row old along with me.
 The best is yet to be;
The last of life, for which the first was made.
 Our times are in His hand
 Who saith, "A whole I planned,
Youth shows but half; Trust God: See all, nor be afraid!"

 Not that, amassing flowers,
 Youth sighed, "Which rose make ours,
Which lily leave and then as best recall?"
 Not that, admiring stars,
 It yearned, "Nor Jove, nor Mars;
Mine be some figured flame which blends, transcends them all!"

 Not for such hopes and fears
 Annulling youth's brief years,

Do I remonstrate: folly wide the mark!
 Rather I prize the doubt
 Low kinds exist without

Finished and finite clods, untroubled by a spark.
 Poor vaunt of life indeed,
 Were man but formed to feed
On joy, to solely seek and find and feast;
 Such feasting ended, then
 As sure an end to men;
Irks care the crop-full bird: Frets doubt the maw-crammed beast?

Rejoice we are allied
To That which doth provide
And not partake, effect and not receive!
A spark disturbs our clod;
Nearer we hold of God
Who gives, than of His tribes that take, I must
believe.
Then, welcome each rebuff
That turns earth's smoothness rough,
Each sting that bids nor sit nor stand but go!
Be our joys three parts pain!
Strive, and hold cheap the stain;
Learn, nor account the pang; dare, never grudge
the throe!
But I need, now as then,
Thee, God, who moldest men;
And since, not even while the whirl was worst,
Did I—to the wheel of life
With shapes and colors rife,
Bound dizzily—mistake my end, to slake Thy
thirst.

—Robert Browning

*W*e all change to some degree each year. The
danger arises when we base our love on change-

able characteristics we found attractive on the companionship level.

—Gary Smalley

*T*he empty-nest stage is a time of gradually slowing down and finding some time on your hands. The question of the day is "What do we do with it?" The empty nest is a time for reinventing your marriage and getting reconnected. It brings the realization of time wasted and of neglecting the person you really care about the most.

—Patrick Morley

*C*ommunication focuses on rebuilding an intimate, personal relationship that's deeper than diapers.

—Patrick Morley

*P*repare your minds for action; be self-controlled; set your hope fully on the grace to be given you when Jesus Christ is revealed.

—1 Peter 1:13

*D*o not store up for yourselves treasures on earth, where moth and rust destroy, and where thieves break in and steal. But store up for yourselves treasures in heaven. . . . For where your treasure is, there your heart will be also.

—*Matthew 6:19-21*

*O*ur deepest desire is to finish well. In 2 Timothy 4:7, the apostle Paul speaks of finishing the race: "I have fought the good fight, I have finished the race, I have kept the faith." We asked ourselves a sobering question: "When we finish the race, what do we want our marriage to look like?" We actually made a list of things we hope will describe us when we've been married fifty-plus years.

—David & Claudia Arp

*S*o we never will build our dream house or be able to retire at fifty-five. We still have each other, and for us that's what is important.

—Husband married for thirty-two years

*F*or everything God created is good, and nothing is to be rejected if it is received with thanksgiving.

—*1 Timothy 4:4*

*T*hey will still bear fruit in old age, they will stay fresh and green, proclaiming, "The LORD is upright; he is my Rock."

—*Psalm 92:14-15*

*T*hanks be to God for his indescribable gift!

—*2 Corinthians 9:15*

*L*ife without thankfulness is lacking in fine perception. Faith without thankfulness lacks strength and fortitude. Every virtue divorced from thankfulness is maimed and limps along the spiritual road.

—*John Henry Jowett*

*G*ratefulness is a sincere appreciation for the benefits you have gained from others.

—*Gary Smalley*

*H*e will wipe every tear from their eyes. There will be no more death or mourning or crying or pain, for the old order of things has passed away.

—Revelation 21:4

*T*hose who sow in tears will reap with songs of joy. He who goes out weeping, carrying seed to sow, will return with songs of joy, carrying sheaves with him.

—Psalm 126:5-6

*T*ypically, most of us expect our mates to retain their original physical and emotional attractive-ness. But a funny thing happens on the way to retirement … we change. And if we change the things our mates once found attractive, we have to replace them with something better.

—Gary Smalley

*K*eep my commands in your heart, for they will prolong your life many years and bring you prosperity.

—Proverbs 3:1-2

The best way to describe the communication in the empty nest stage is to call it *the key to happiness.* Ways to improve communication include listening, asking questions, expressing life verbally, and commenting on each other's interests.

—Patrick Morley

Even to your old age and gray hairs I am he, I am he who will sustain you. I have made you and I will carry you; I will sustain you and I will rescue you.

—Isaiah 46:4

Many waters cannot quench love; rivers cannot wash it away. If one were to give all the wealth of his house for love, it would be utterly scorned.

—*Song of Songs 8:7*

There is a time for everything, and a season for every activity under heaven.

—*Ecclesiastes 3:1*

*L*ove's sweetest adventure is the one we will share tomorrow!

—Beth Swanson

*A*nd now these three remain: faith, hope and love. But the greatest of these is love.

—1 Corinthians 13:1

*D*o not let your hearts be troubled. Trust in God; trust also in me. In my Father's house are many rooms; if it were not so, I would have told you. I am going there to prepare a place for you. And if I go and prepare a place for you, I will come back and take you to be with me that you also may be where I am.
You know the way to the place where I am going."
Thomas said to him, "Lord, we don't know where you are going, so how can we know the way?"
Jesus answered, "I am the way and the truth and the life. No one comes to the Father except through me."

—John 14:1–6

Sources

Arp, David and Claudia. *10 Great Dates to Revitalize Your Marriage.* Grand Rapids: Zondervan Publishing House, 1997.

Arp, David and Claudia. *The Second Half of Marriage.* Grand Rapids: Zondervan Publishing House, 1996.

Barnes, Robert and Rosemary. *Rock-Solid Marriage.* Grand Rapids: Zondervan Publishing House, 1993.

Barnes, Robert and Rosemary. *We Need To Talk.* Grand Rapids: Zondervan Publishing House, 1994.

Brant, Henry R. *I Want My Marriage To Be Better.* Grand Rapids: Zondervan Publishing House, 1976.

Couple's Devotional Bible. Grand Rapids: Zondervan Publishing House, 1994.

God's Wisdom for Women Devotional Calendar. Grand Rapids: Zondervan Publishing House, 1997.

Hybels, Bill and Lynne. *Fit To Be Tied.* Grand Rapids: Zondervan Publishing House, 1993.

Johnson, Barbara. *Boomerang Joy Daybreak.* Grand Rapids: Zondervan Publishing House, 1998.

Liawtuad, Marian V. (Editor). *Swatting the Mosquitoes of Marriage.* Grand Rapids: Zondervan Publishing House, 1994.

Morley, Patrick. *What Husbands Wish Their Wives Knew About Men.* Grand Rapids: Zondervan Publishing House, 1997.

Osborne, Cecil. *The Art of Understanding Your Mate.* Grand Rapids: Zondervan Publishing House, 1970.

Parrott, Drs. Les and Leslie. *Saving Your Marriage Before It Starts.* Grand Rapids: Zondervan Publishing House, 1995.

Parrott, Drs. Les and Leslie. *Love Is . . . .* Grand Rapids: Zondervan Publishing House, 1999.

Product Concept Designs: *Letters To My Love.* Grand Rapids: Zondervan Publishing House, 1996.

Smalley, Gary. *For Better or For Best.* Grand Rapids: Zondervan Publishing House, 1987.

Smalley, Gary. *Hidden Keys of a Loving, Lasting Marriage.* Grand Rapids: Zondervan Publishing House, 1993.

Smalley, Gary. *The Joy of Committed Love.* Grand Rapids: Zondervan Publishing House, 1984.

Stanley, Charles. *A Touch of His Goodness.* Grand Rapids: Zondervan Publishing House, 1998.

Wheat, Ed. *The First Years of Forever.* Grand Rapids: Zondervan Publishing House, 1988.

Women's Devotional Bible. Grand Rapids: Zondervan Publishing House, 1990.